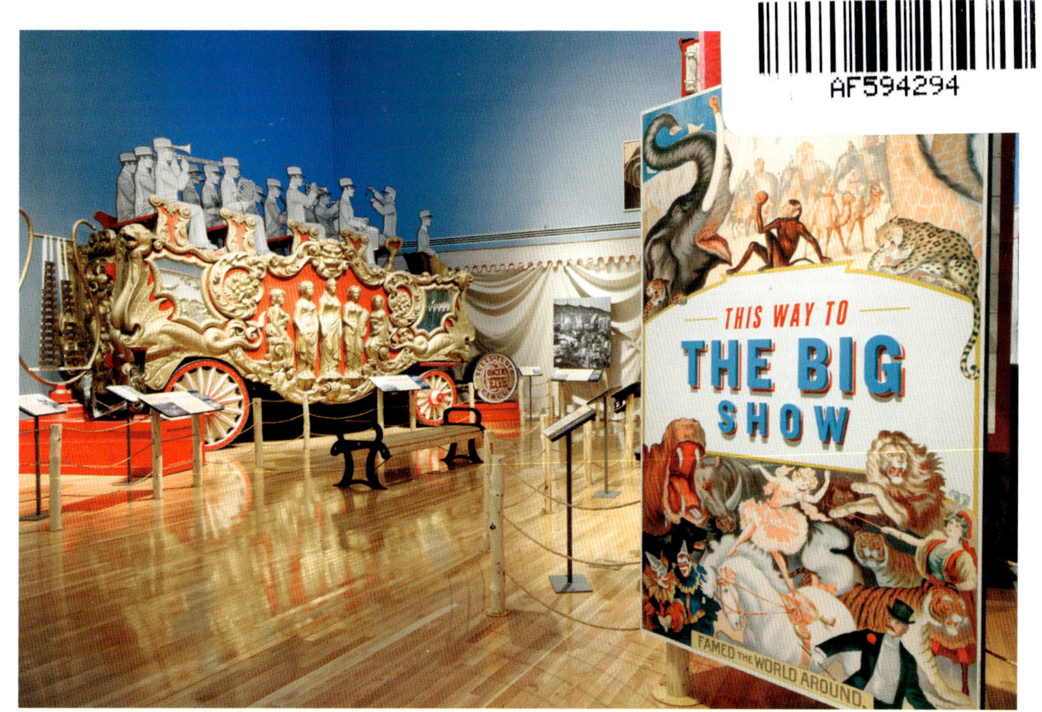

The Ringling

VISITOR GUIDE

DAVID A. BERRY

SCALA

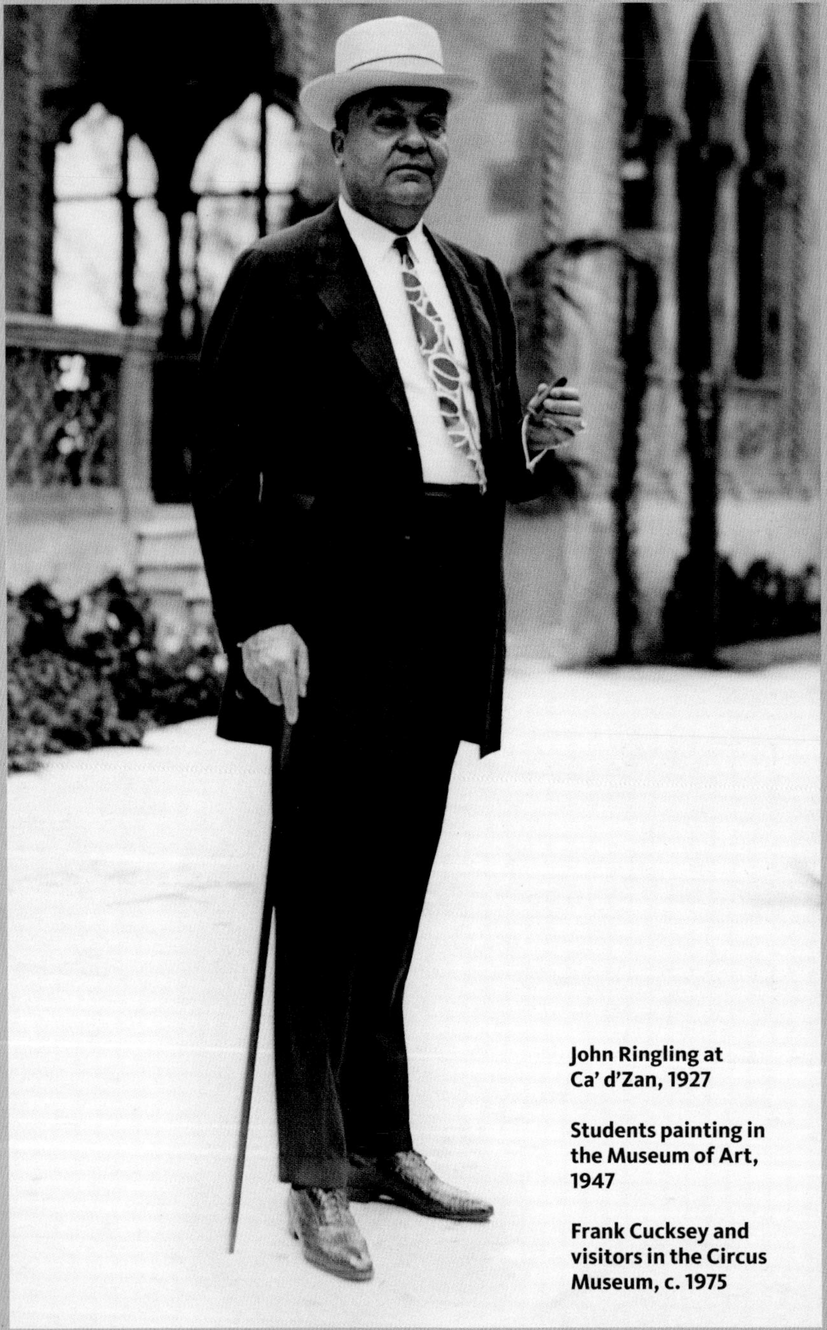

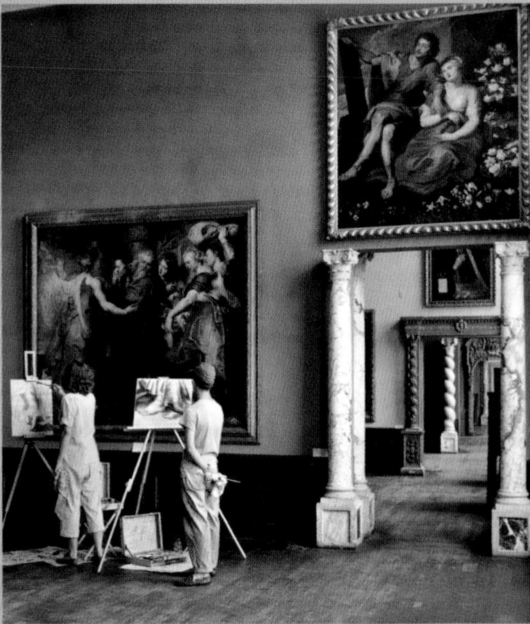

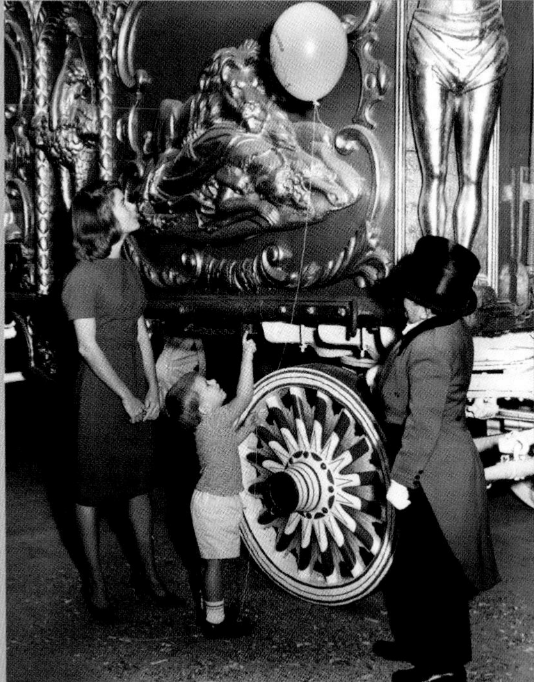

John Ringling at Ca' d'Zan, 1927

Students painting in the Museum of Art, 1947

Frank Cucksey and visitors in the Circus Museum, c. 1975

CONTENTS

INTRODUCTION

The Ringling is an institution unlike any other. It combines outstanding art and circus museums with a historic mansion and theater, all set amid beautiful bayfront gardens. A sense of spectacle pervades The Ringling, reflecting the personality of the great showman who founded it.

The history of The Ringling begins in 1911, when circus owner John Ringling and his wife, Mable Burton Ringling, purchased property in Sarasota, Florida. Previously owned by Charles Thompson, a one-time manager of the Buffalo Bill Wild West Show, the property consisted of a house, known as Palms Elysian, and twenty acres of grounds on the shores of Sarasota Bay.

The Ringlings began construction on a new winter residence to replace Palms Elysian in 1924. Completed two years later, the mansion, known as Ca' d'Zan (meaning "House of John" in Venetian dialect), was used to entertain family and friends, as well as wealthy investors interested in supporting John's efforts to transform Sarasota from a sleepy fishing village into a fashionable resort town.

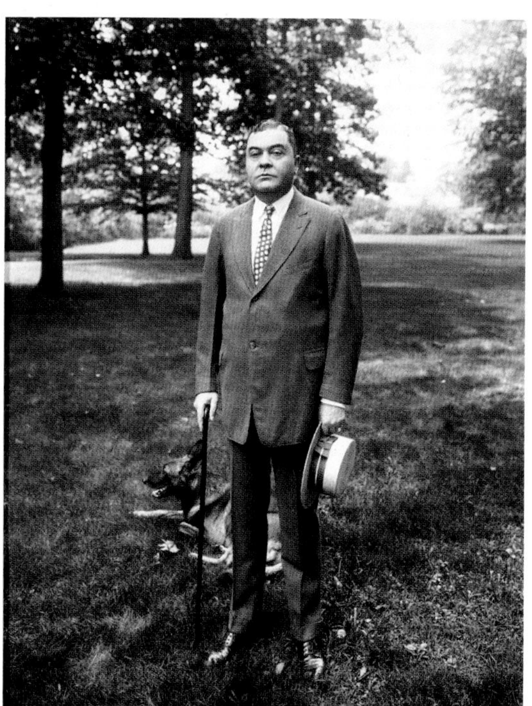

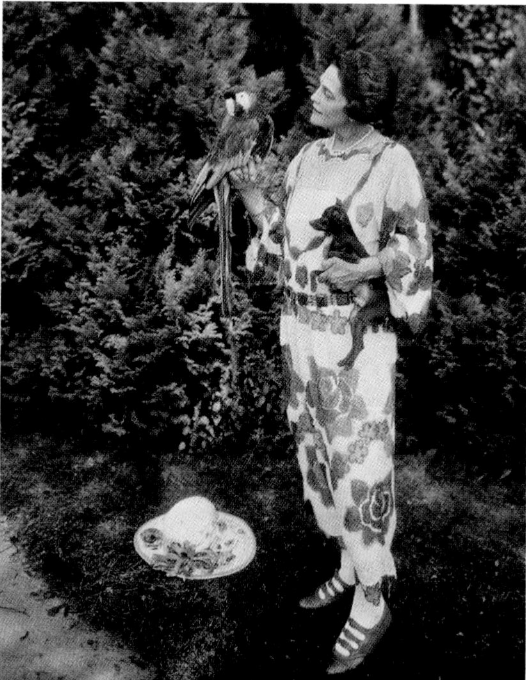

John Ringling, c. 1927
John Ringling's fortune was based not only on the circus, but also on other investments, including oil, railroads, and real estate.

Mable Ringling, c. 1927
Mable Ringling shared her husband's interests in art, culture, and travel, and was actively involved in his various projects around Sarasota.

Ca' d'Zan, 1927

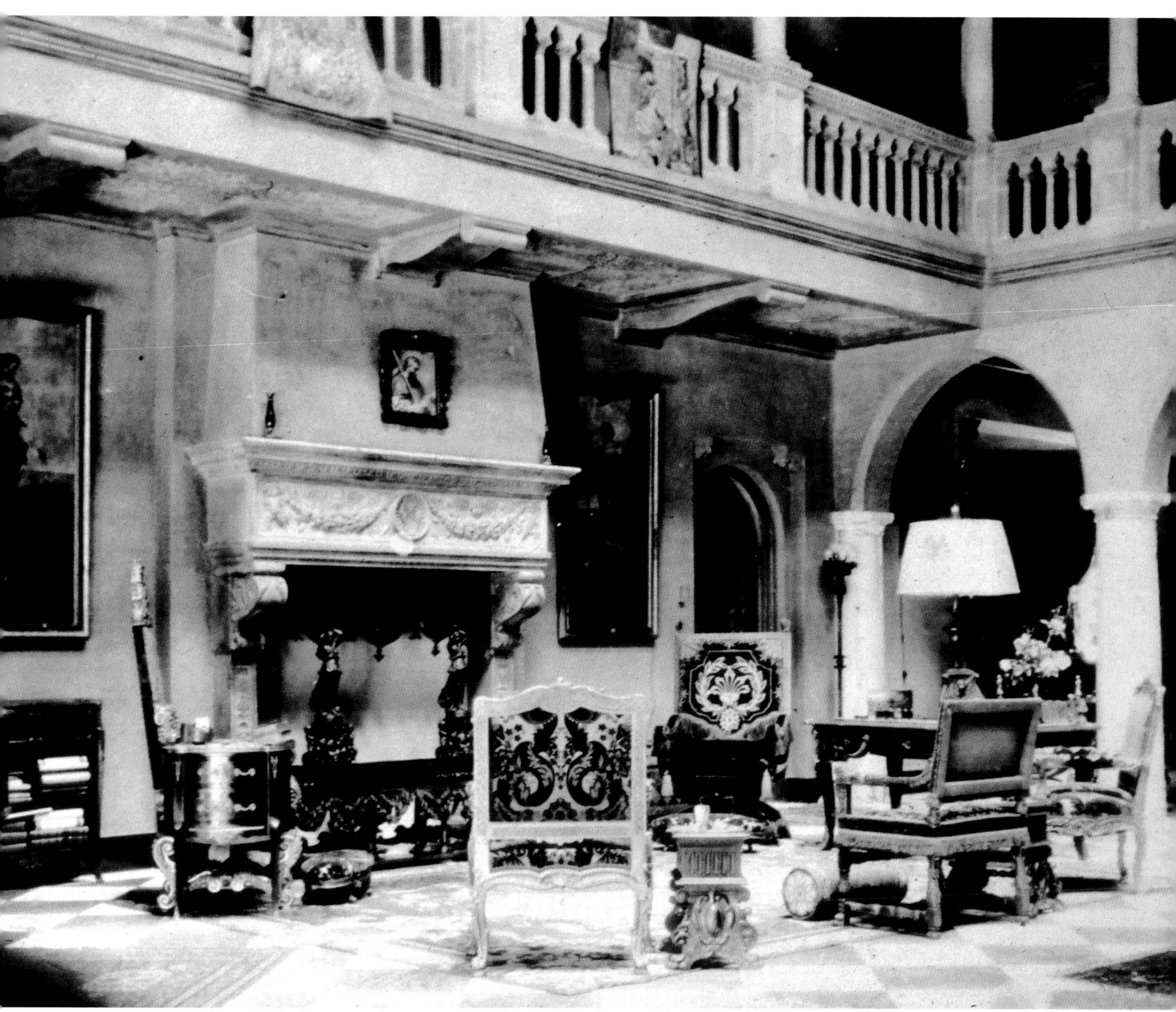

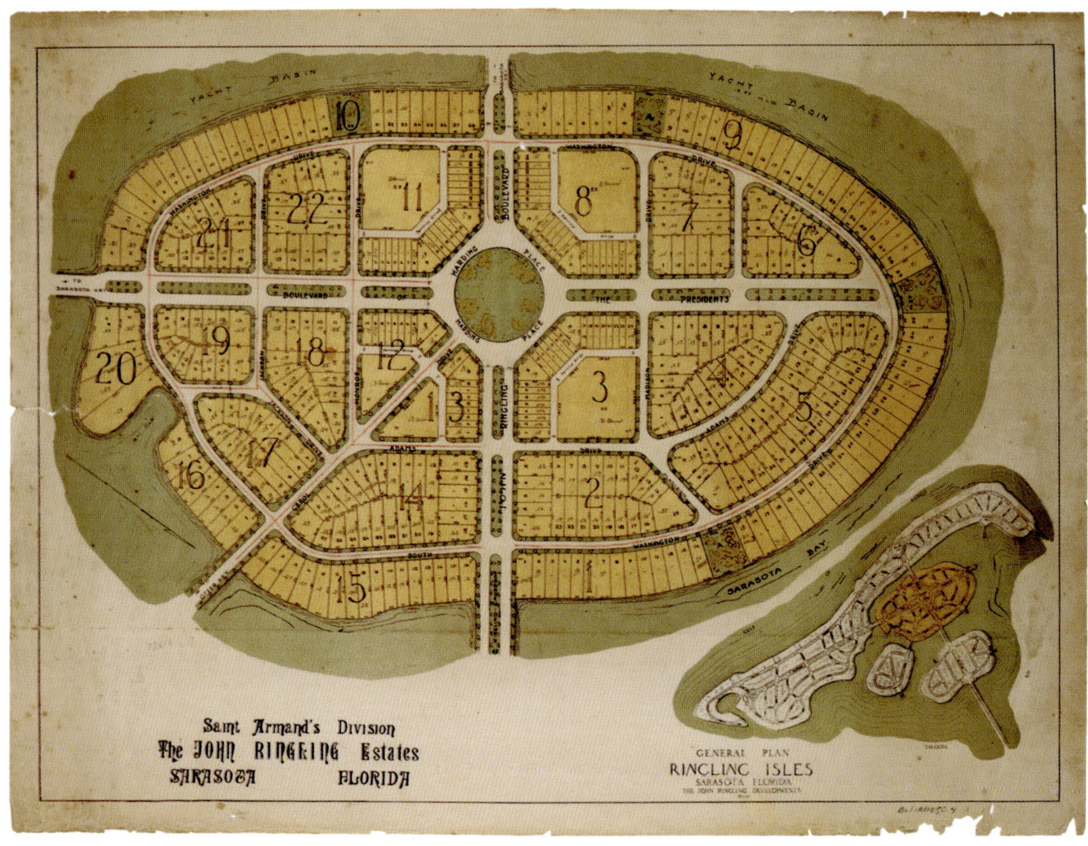

John Watson, plan of Ringling Isles, 1924
John Ringling bought and developed land on the keys across Sarasota Bay. The shopping district known today as St. Armands Circle was one of his projects.

To this end, John established an art museum inspired by those he had seen on trips to Europe in search of new circus acts. The museum opened in the early 1930s, displaying an exceptional collection of Old Master paintings, sculptures, decorative arts, and antiquities.

John's health and fortune declined in the last years of his life. Upon his death in 1936, the mansion and museum were bequeathed to the State of Florida. They were accepted after his estate was settled in 1946.

Arthur Everett "Chick" Austin, Jr. served as The Ringling's first director. He opened the mansion to the public, enriched the art museum with new acquisitions, established a circus museum in honor of John Ringling, and installed an eighteenth-century theater from Asolo, Italy. In doing so, he defined the scope of The Ringling as it is today.

Stewardship of The Ringling passed to Florida State University (FSU) in 2000. A number of new buildings were added in the years that followed, including a Visitor Pavilion and Education Center housing a conservation laboratory and art library. Together with the FSU Center for the Performing Arts across the street, The Ringling is now one of the largest university arts complexes in the United States.

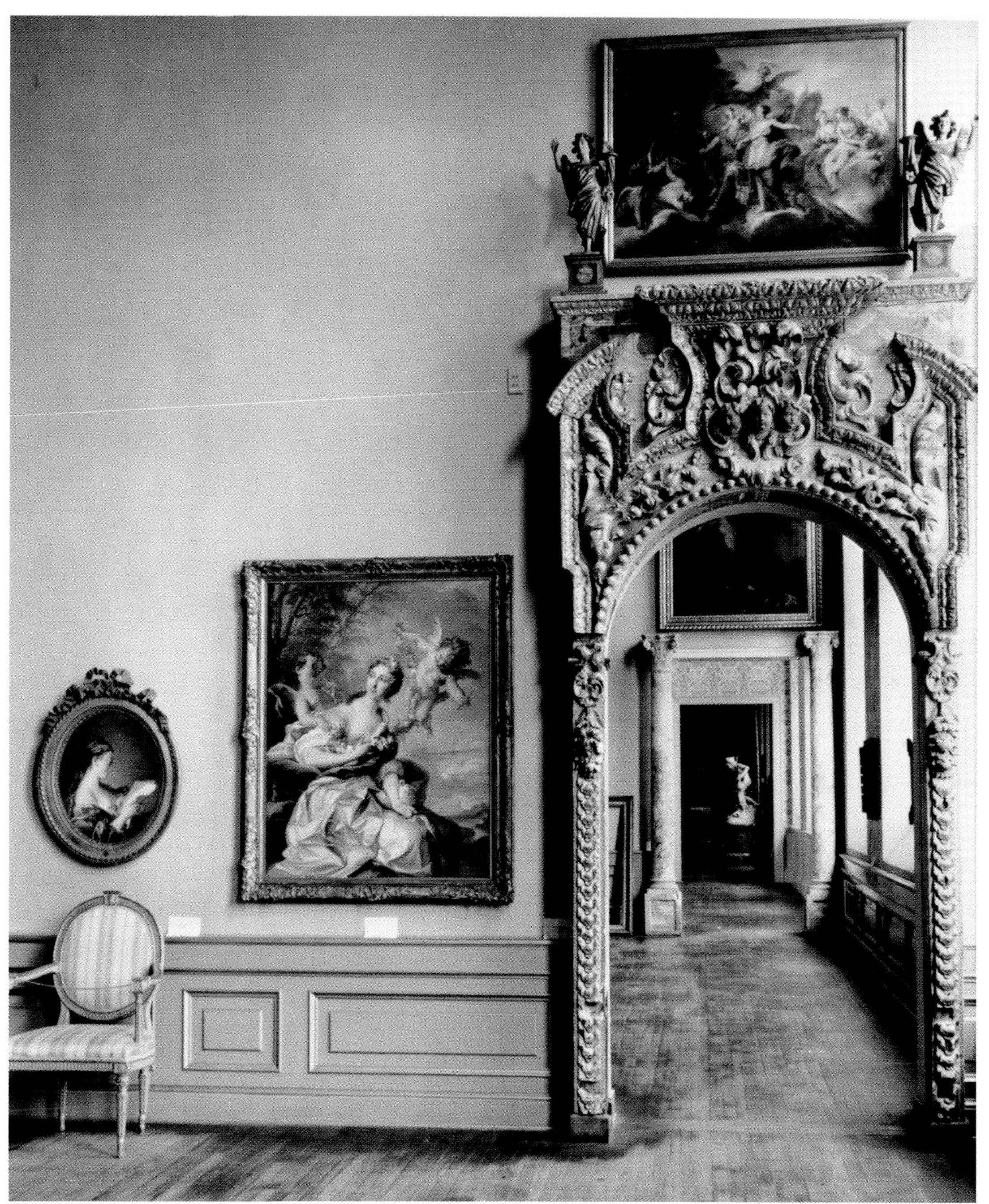

Museum of Art, c. 1930

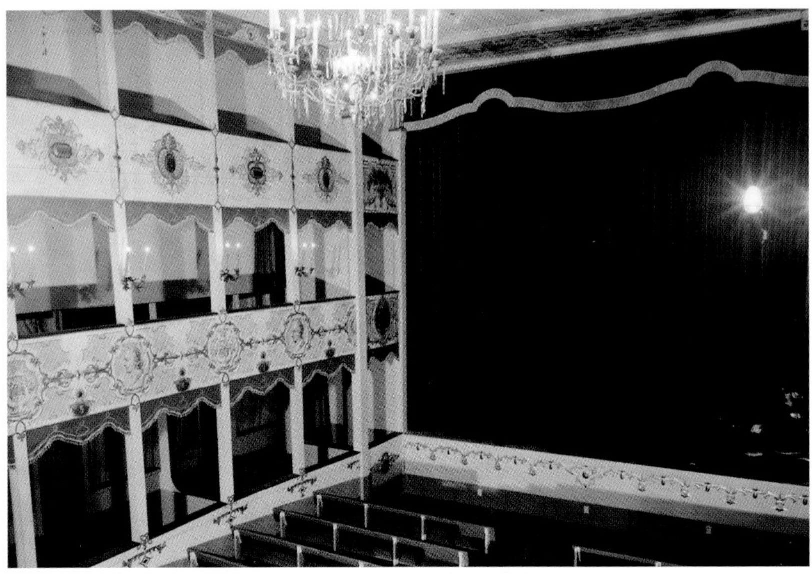

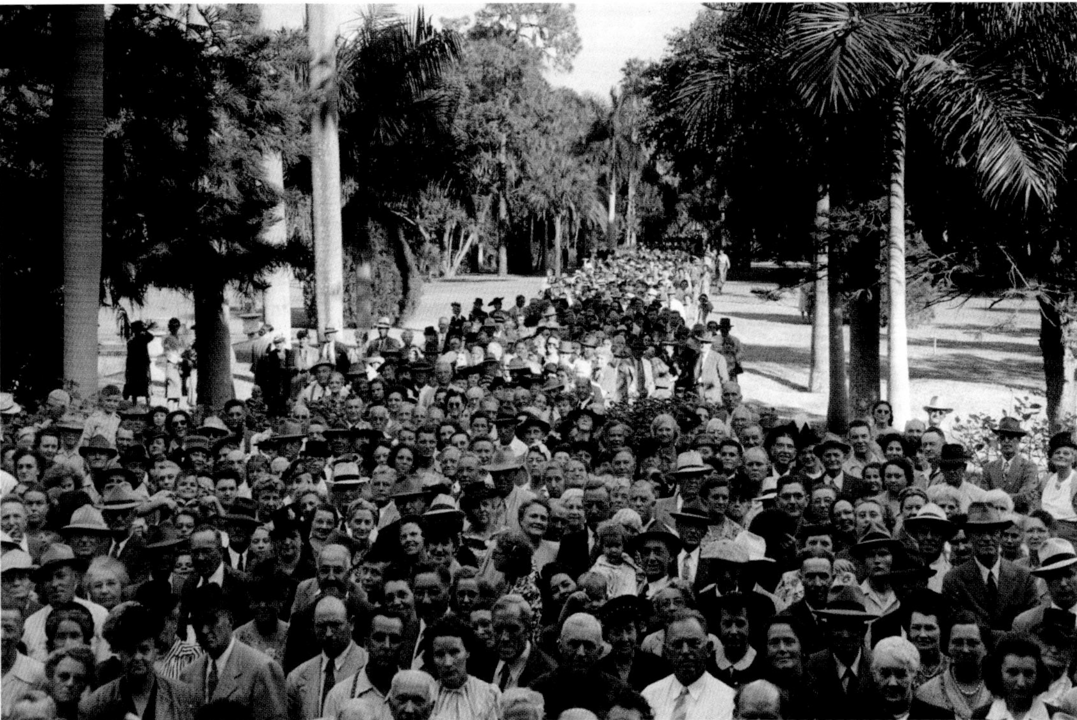

Historic Asolo Theater, 1952

Opening day of Ca' d'Zan, 1946

Chick Austin and students from Florida State University, 1948

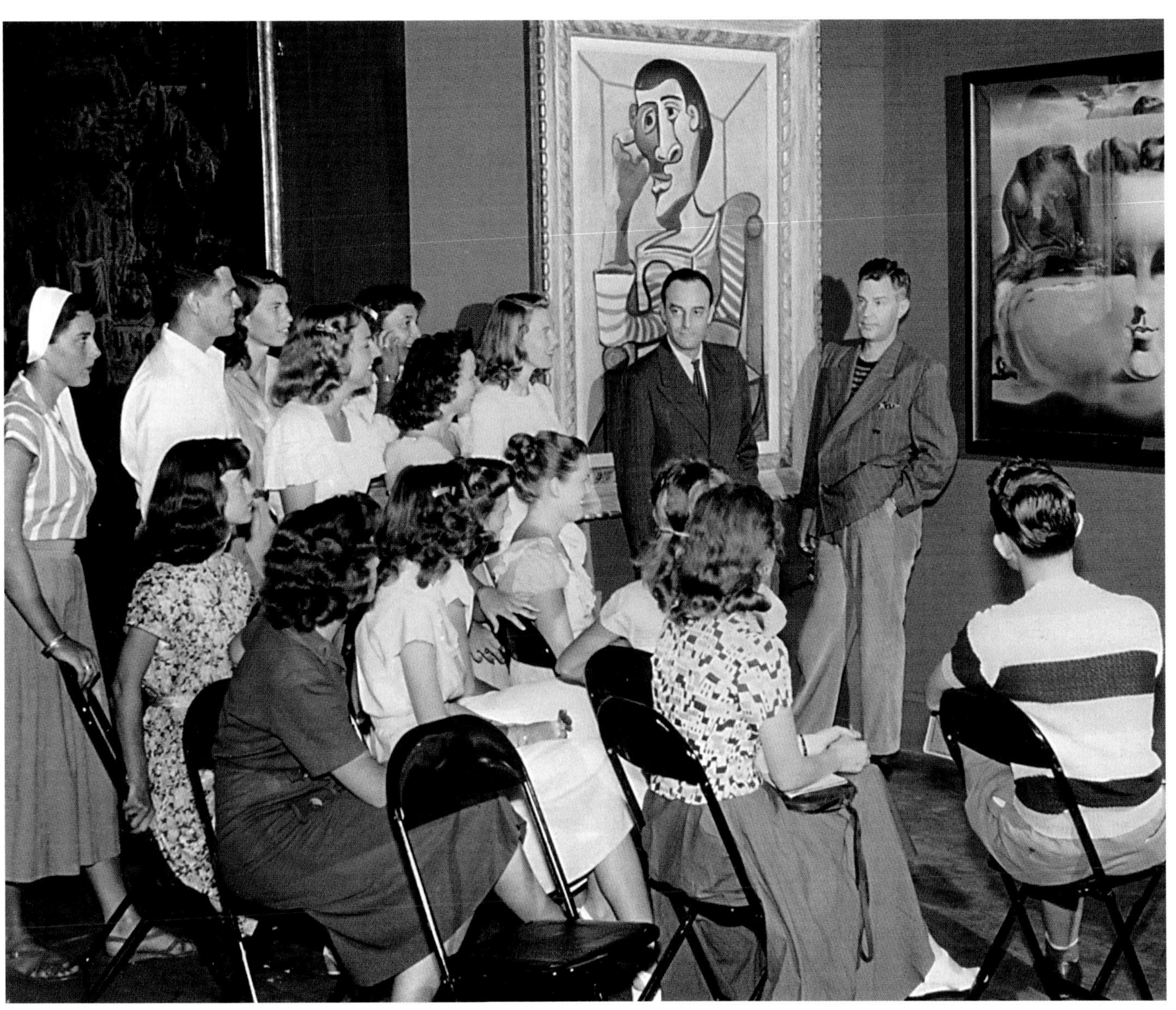

Circus Museum, c. 1948

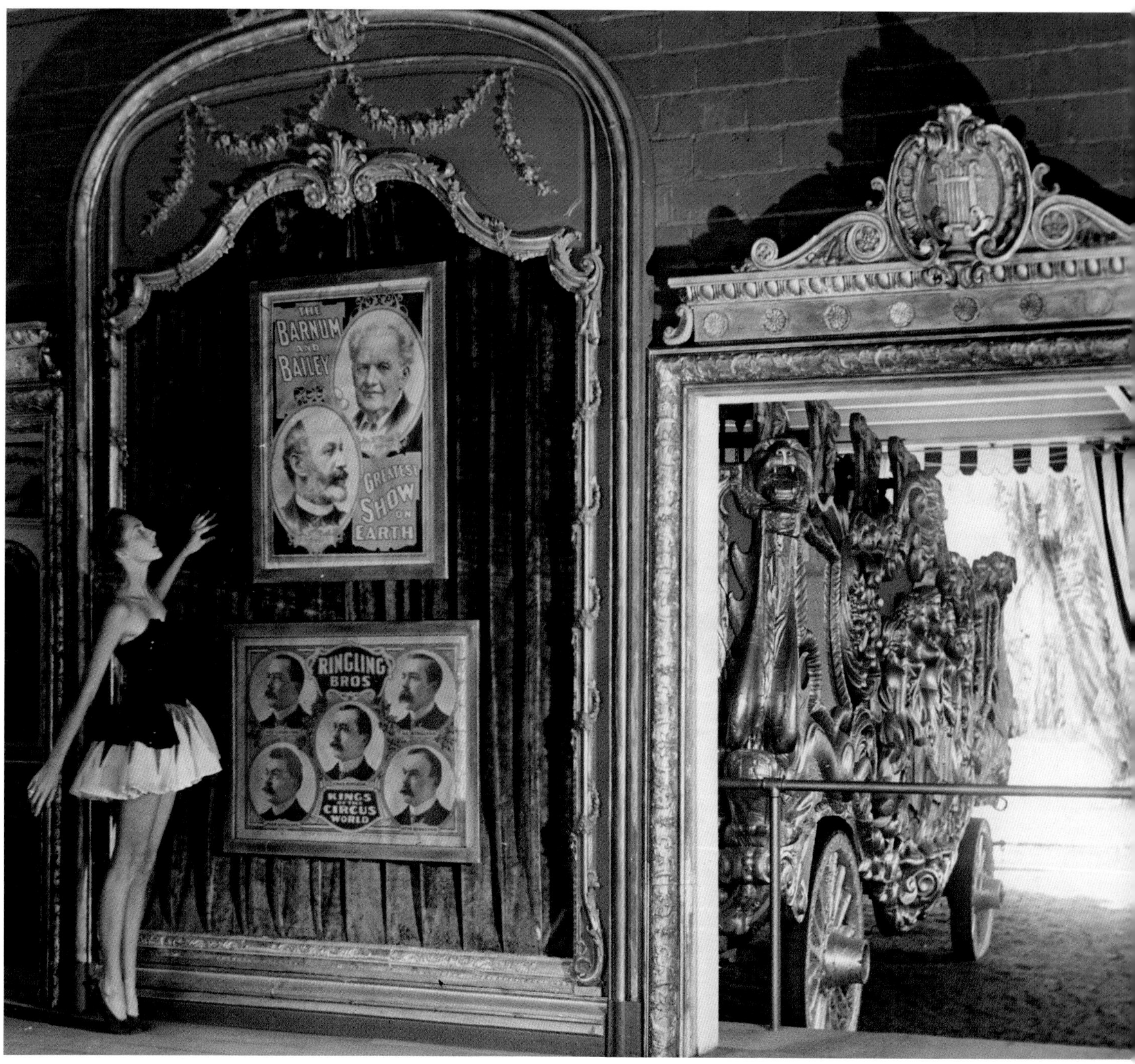

RINGLING BROS. CIRCUS

John Ringling and four of his brothers (Albert, Alfred, Charles, and Otto) founded the Ringling Bros. Circus in Baraboo, Wisconsin, in 1884. While John first performed as a clown, he later managed the transport of the circus, which shifted from wagon to rail in 1890. The railroad transformed the Ringling Bros. Circus into a national phenomenon rivaling the renowned Barnum & Bailey Circus, which the Ringlings acquired in 1907. The two circuses ran as separate units until 1919, when they combined to form the Ringling Bros. and Barnum & Bailey Circus, "The Greatest Show on Earth." Upon John's death in 1936, control of the circus passed to his nephew and namesake, John Ringling North, who sold it to the Feld family in 1967.

Courier Lithograph Company, Ringling Bros. Circus poster, 1898

John Ringling on the circus lot, 1928

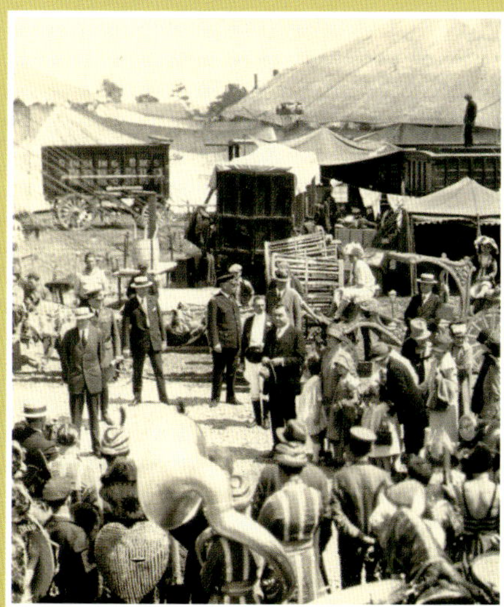

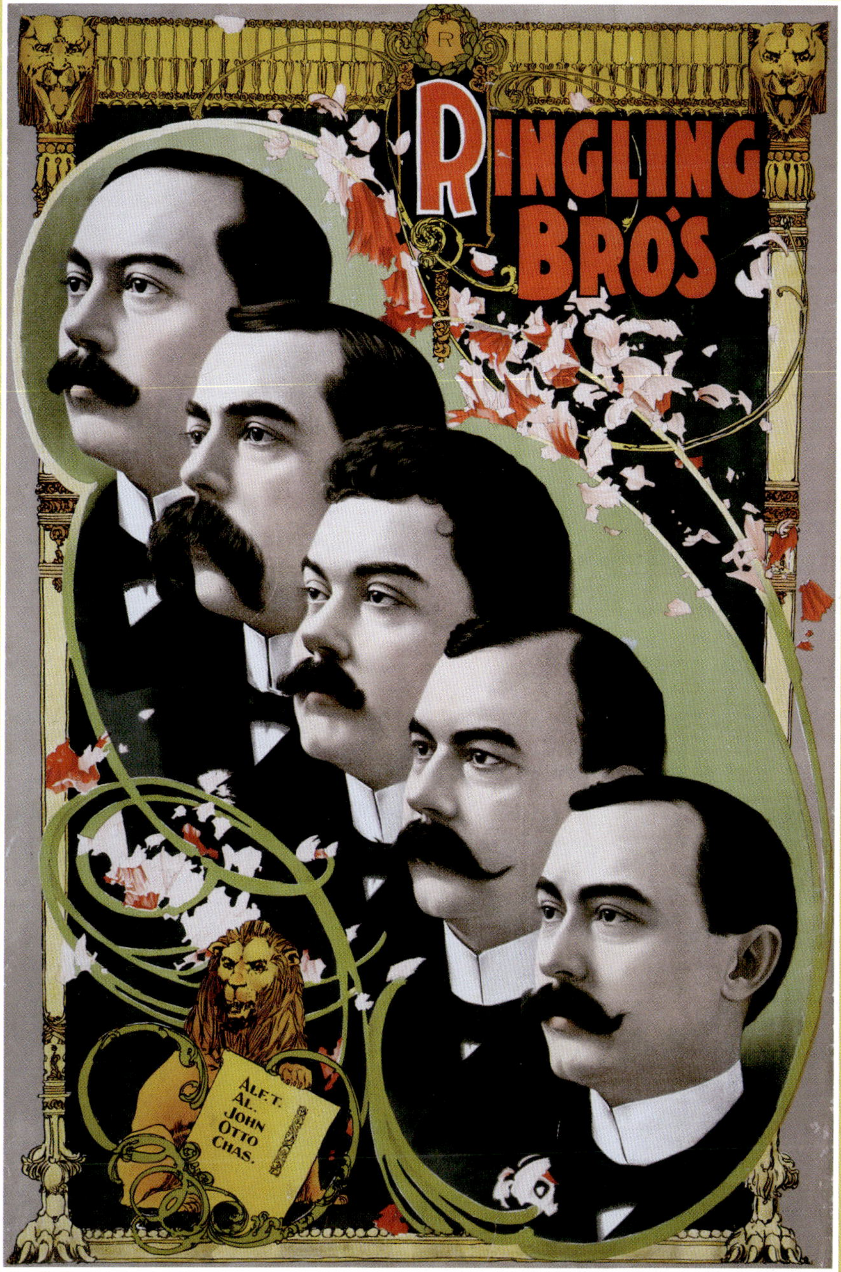

CA' D'ZAN

Earl Purdy (for Dwight James Baum), architectural renderings of Ca' d'Zan, c. 1924

Architect Dwight James Baum designed the Ringlings' winter residence, Ca' d'Zan, in the style of the Venetian Gothic palaces that John and Mable had admired on their trips to Italy. Built between 1924 and 1926 at a cost of $1.5 million, the mansion occupies 36,000 square feet and comprises fifty-six rooms. It was constructed of fine materials, including colored marble, glazed terracotta, and stained glass, and decorated by skilled artisans such as Willy Pogány, a well-known book illustrator and set designer for ballets, operas, and films. While it was furnished with antiques, such as

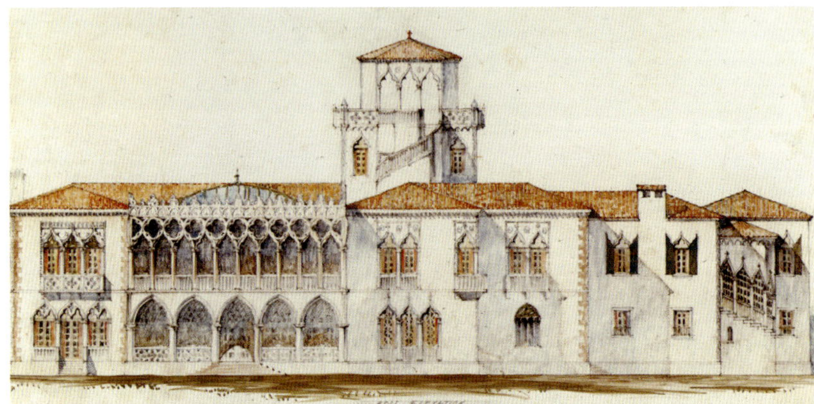

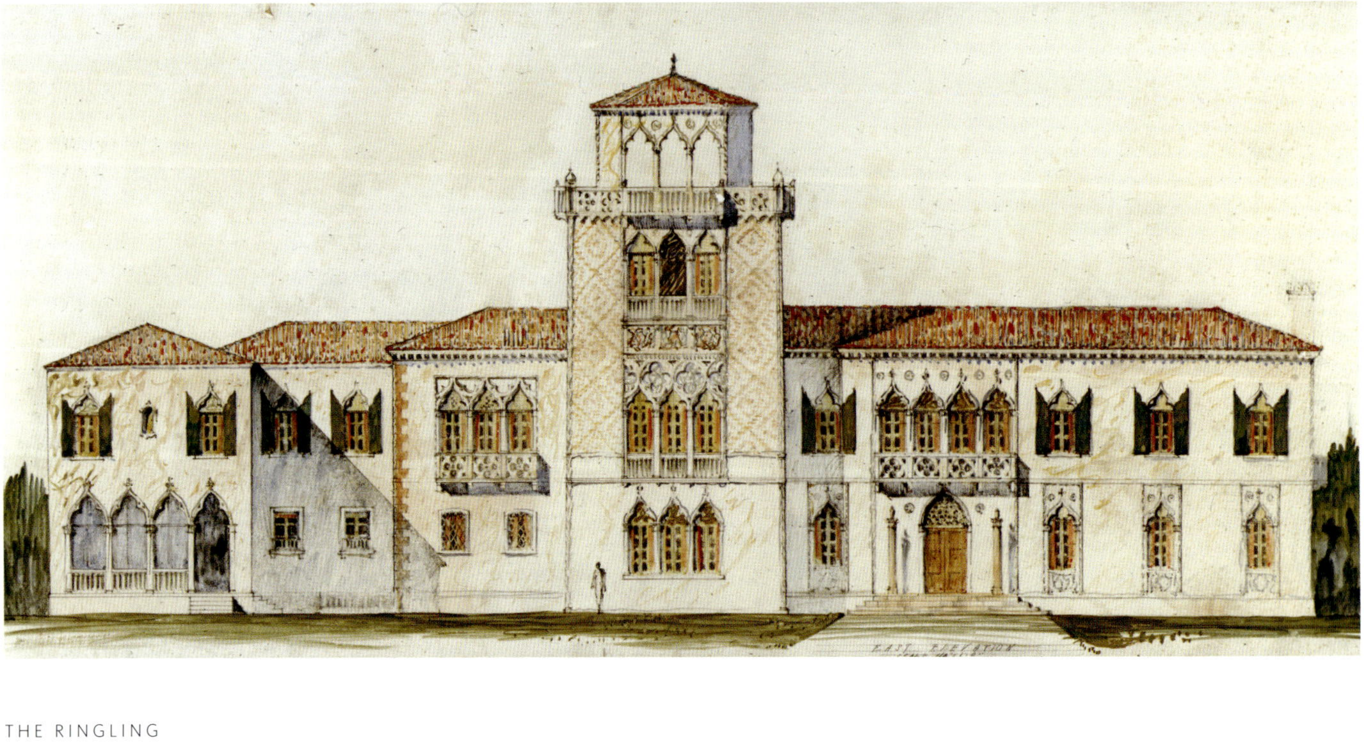

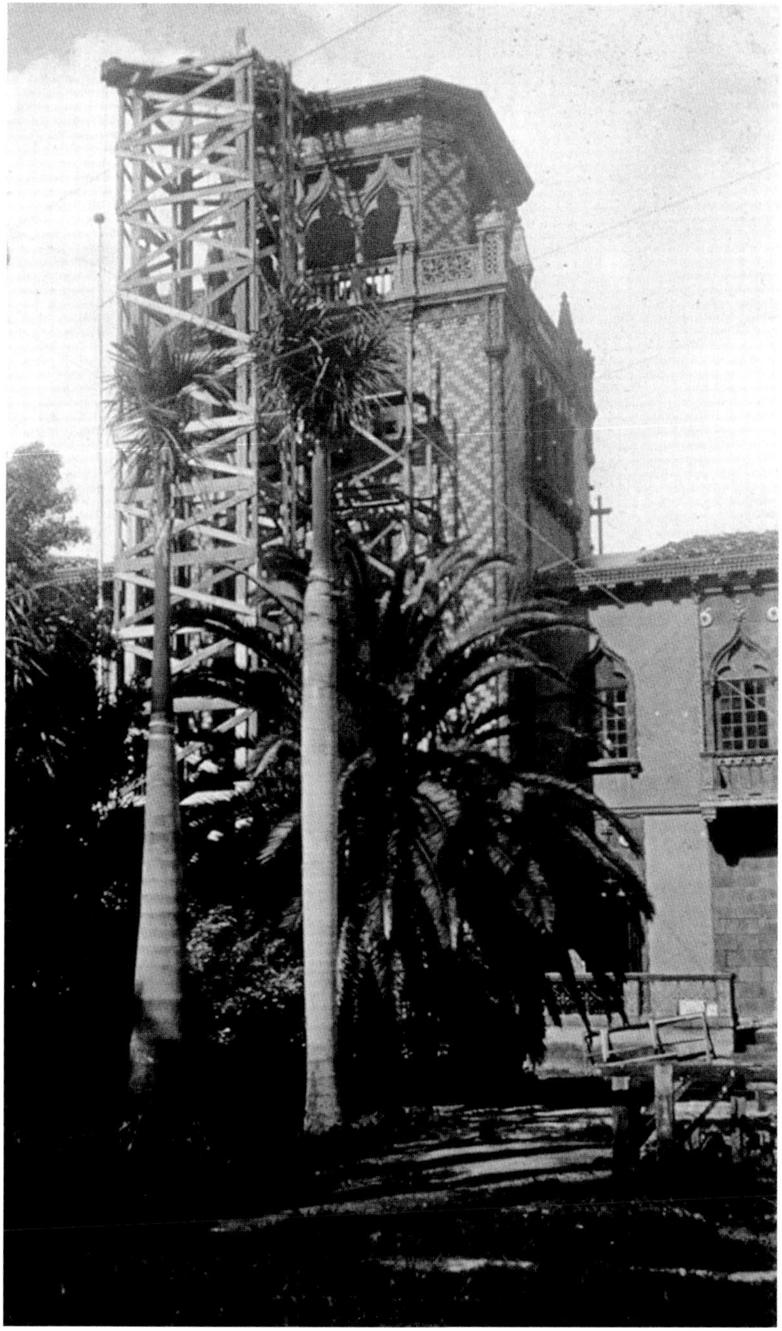

Ca' d'Zan under construction, c. 1925

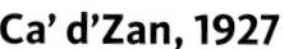

Ca' d'Zan, 1927

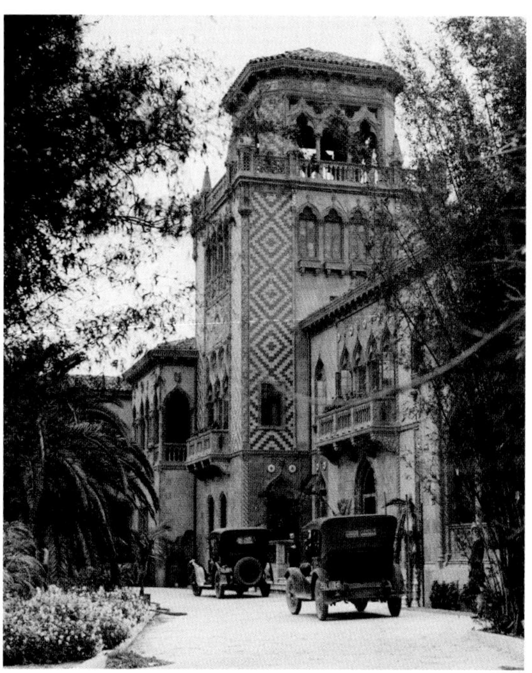

seventeenth-century tapestries, it was also fitted with modern conveniences, including one of the first private elevators in Florida.

The Ringlings used Ca' d'Zan to entertain family and friends, including politicians and celebrities such as New York City mayor Jimmy Walker and Hollywood actress Billie Burke. Guests sipped cocktails at an Art Deco bar bought by John Ringling in 1925 from the Cicardi Restaurant in St. Louis, Missouri. They danced in the ballroom and court to music played on an Aeolian organ and Steinway grand piano. When the weather was good, parties were held on the large waterfront terrace, which doubled as a dance floor able to accommodate as many as 500 people. A band would perform on one of John's yachts, moored at the dock.

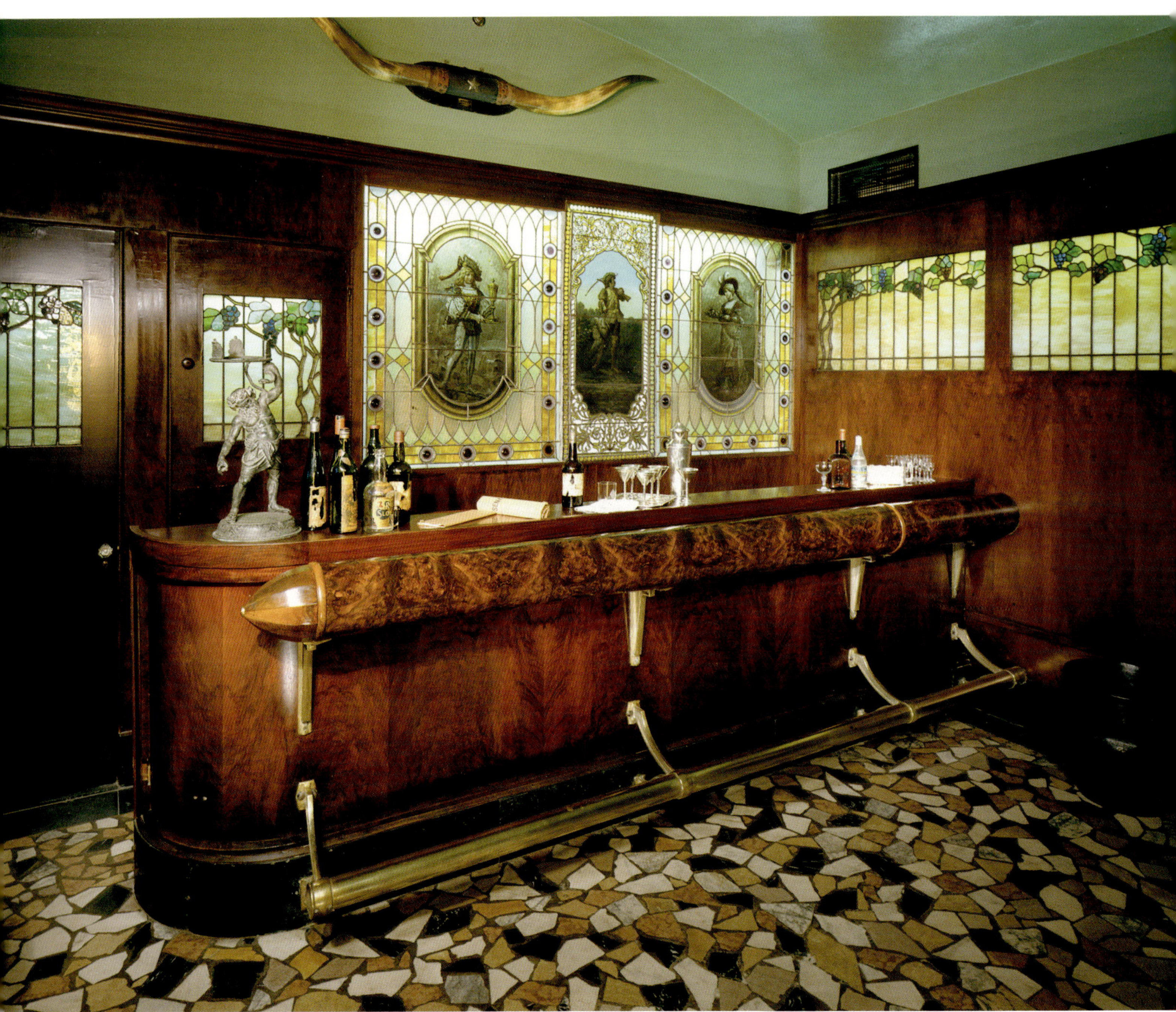

Taproom of Ca' d'Zan
During the Prohibition era (1920–1933), the liquor served here was stored in a vault hidden behind a false wall two floors above.

Social gathering at Ca' d'Zan, c. 1926
Mable Ringling is shown here seated with her mother and sisters.

Overleaf:
Ballroom of Ca' d'Zan
The ceiling of this room depicts scenes of dancing couples from around the world painted in 1926 by artist Willy Pogány.

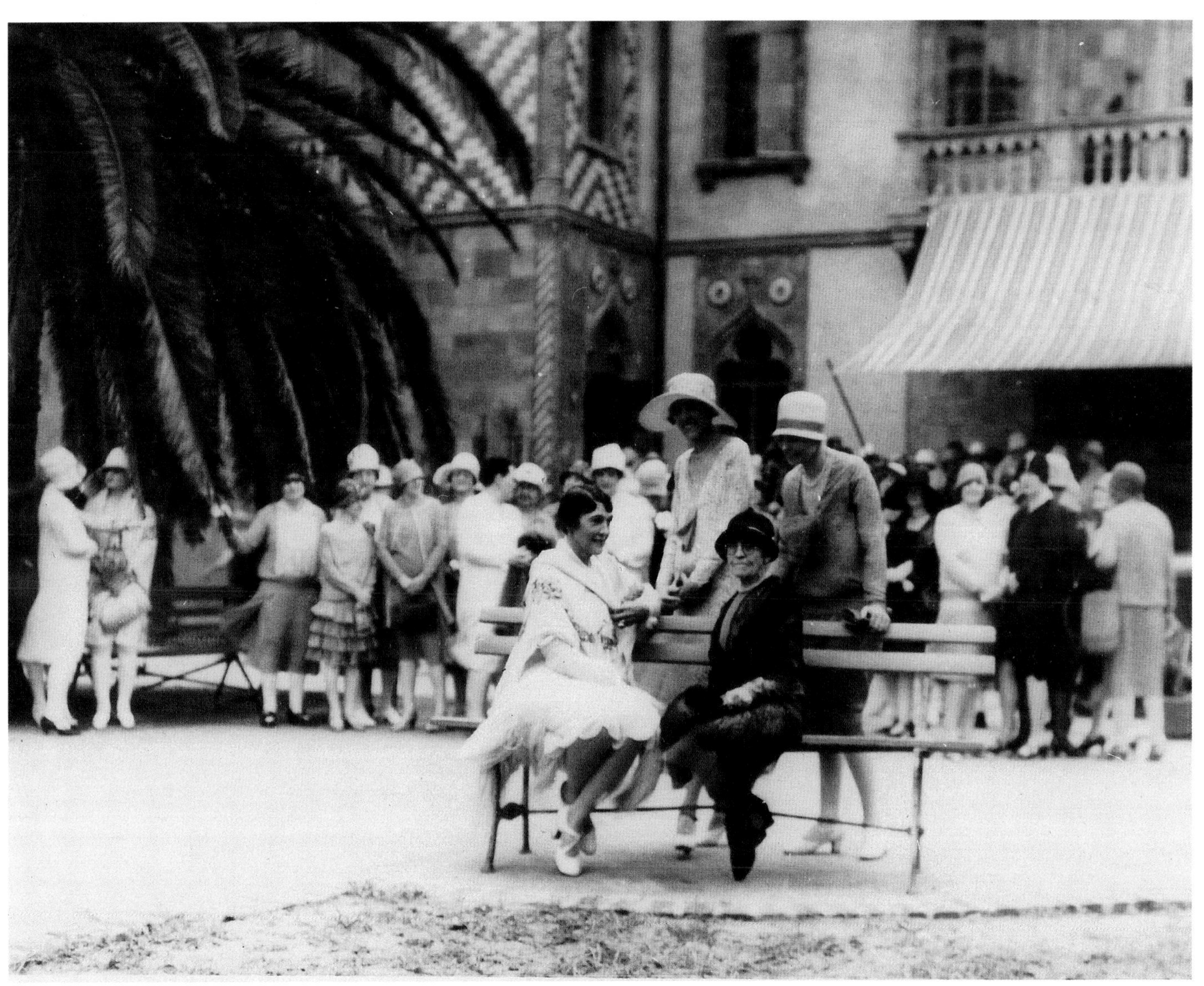

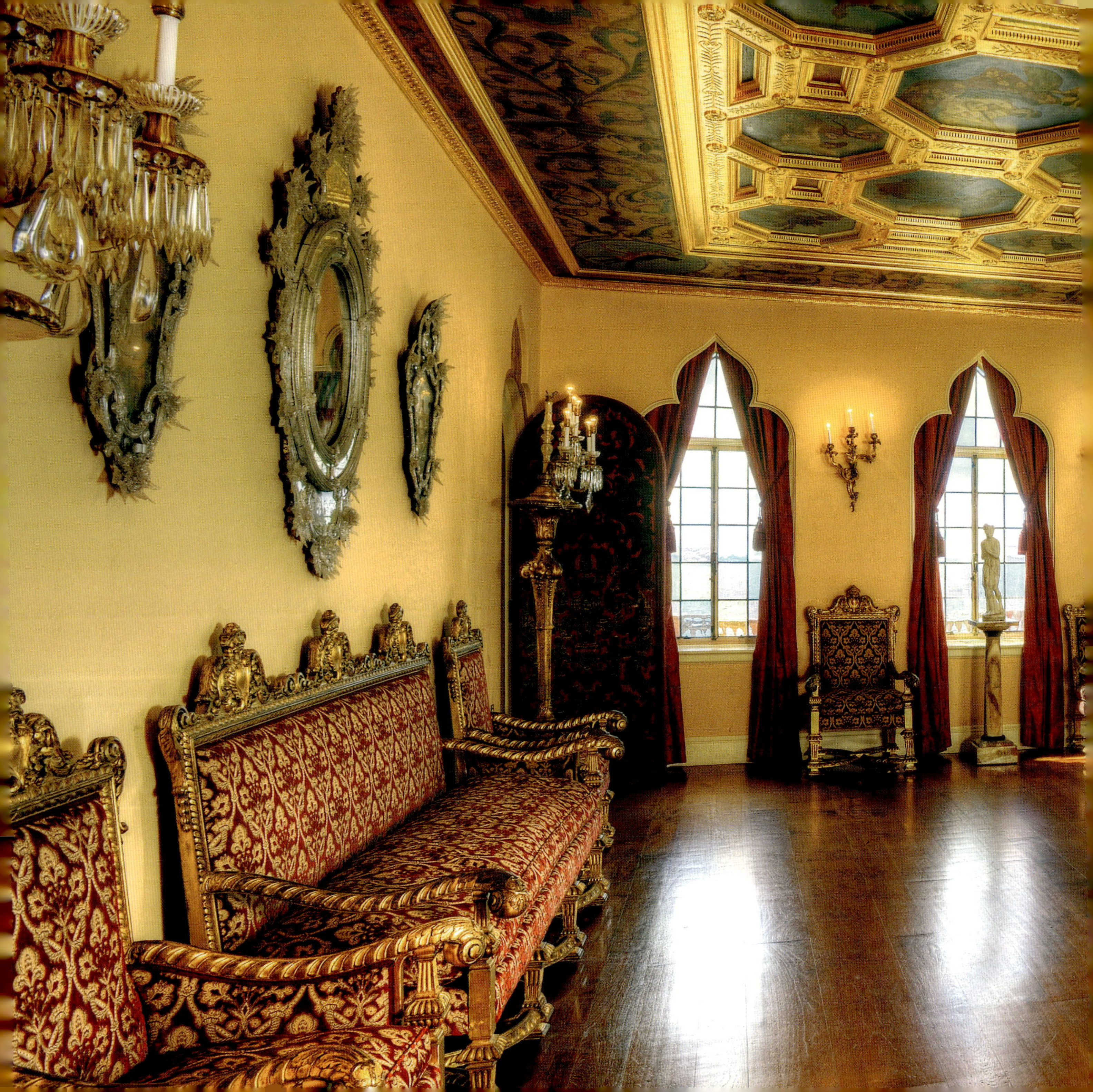

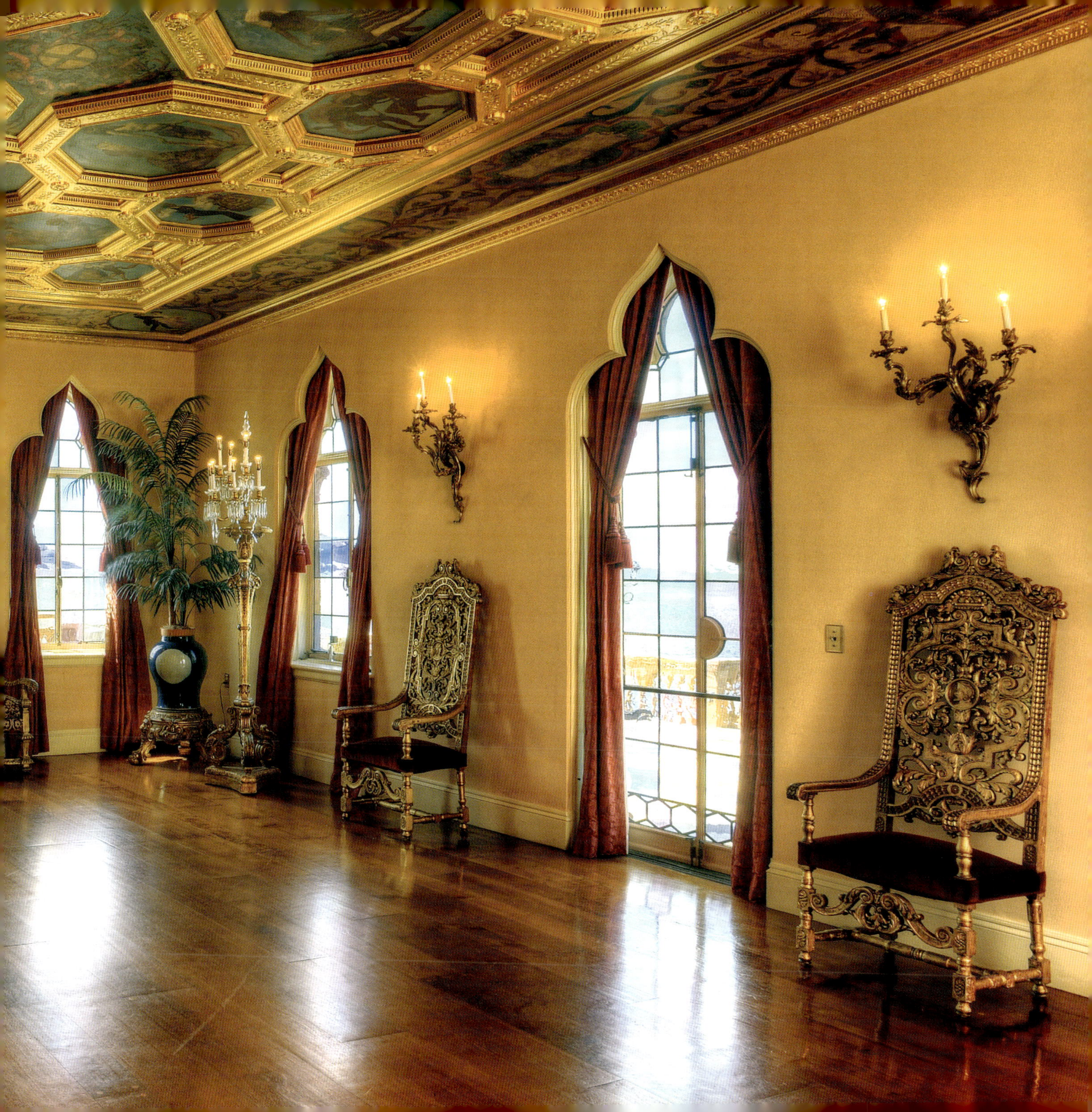

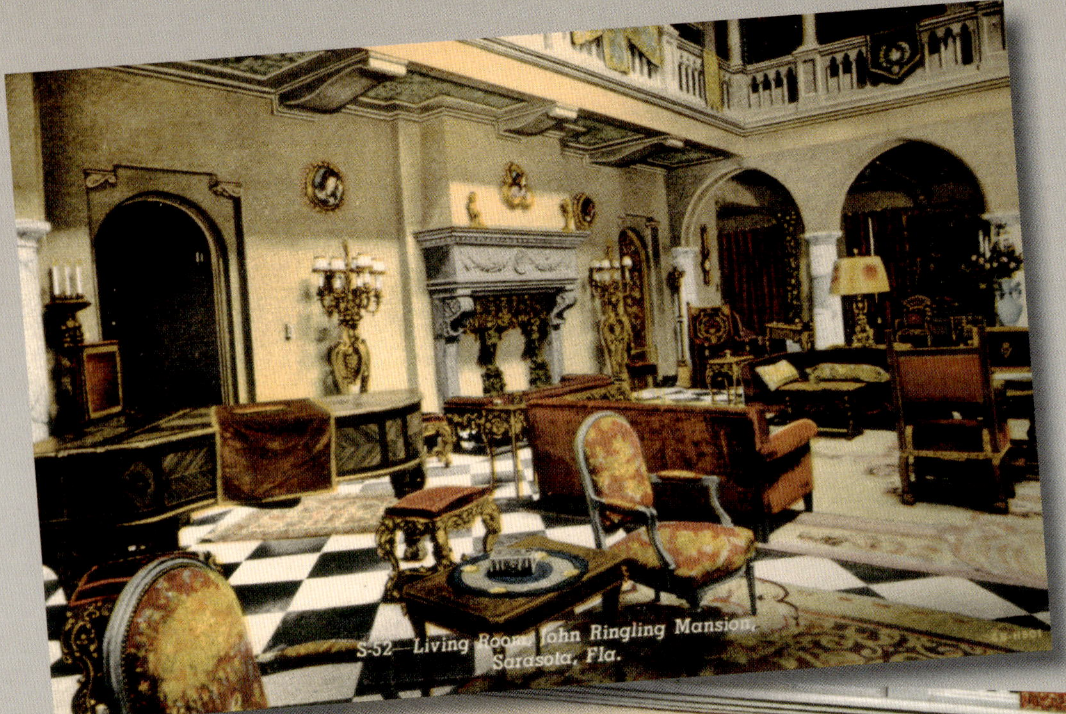

John Ringling's yacht, *Zalophus*, 1920s
This 125-foot yacht sunk in 1930 a mile or so off of Lido Beach.

Postcards of Ca' d'Zan, 1950s
These postcards feature views of the court where the Ringlings entertained family and friends.

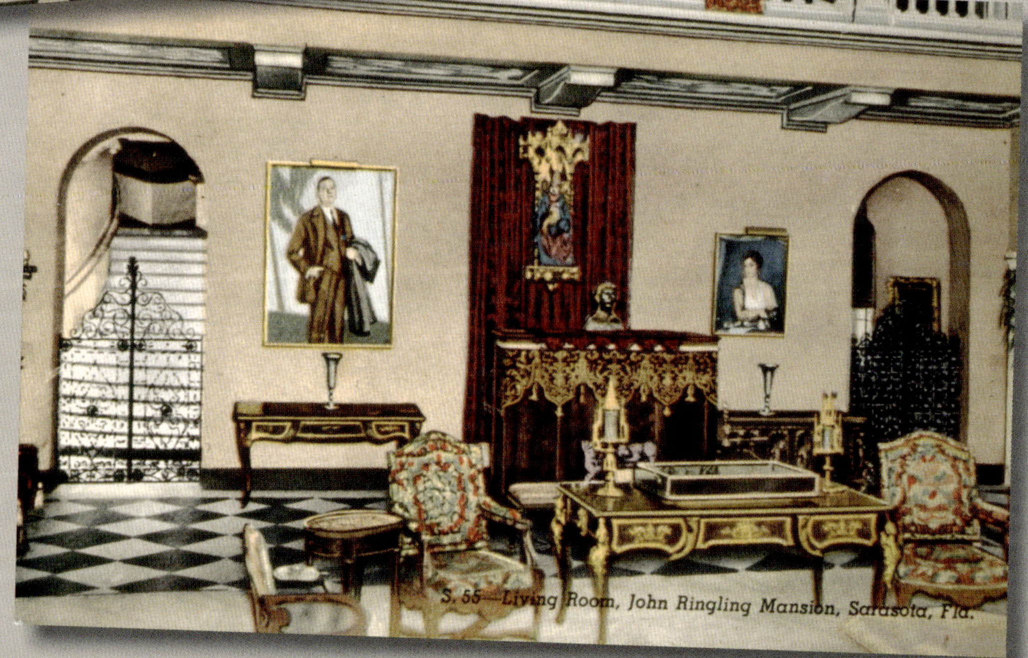

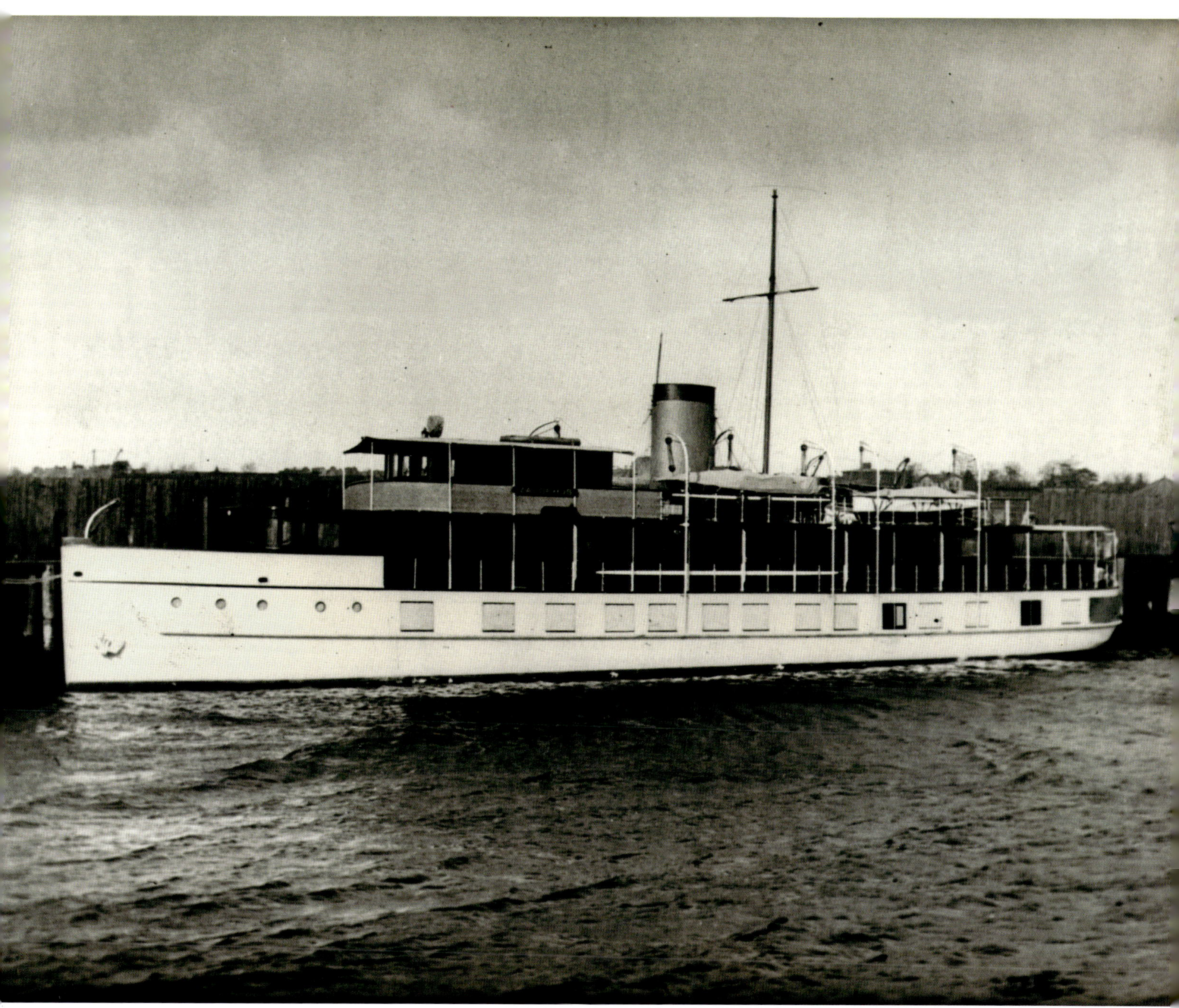

MUSEUM OF ART

John Ringling first expressed the idea of establishing an art museum in Sarasota while on a trip to Italy in 1925. To realize his vision, he spent the next six years amassing a remarkable collection of European paintings from the late Middle Ages to the nineteenth century. The most significant of these are the Italian and Flemish Baroque paintings, the majority of which were acquired at auctions in New York City and London.

John supplemented his collection of paintings with paneled rooms and other architectural elements from the Astor and Huntington Mansions in New York City, as well as more than 300 works of medieval and Renaissance art from Alva Vanderbilt Belmont,

John Ringling at an auction in London, 1928

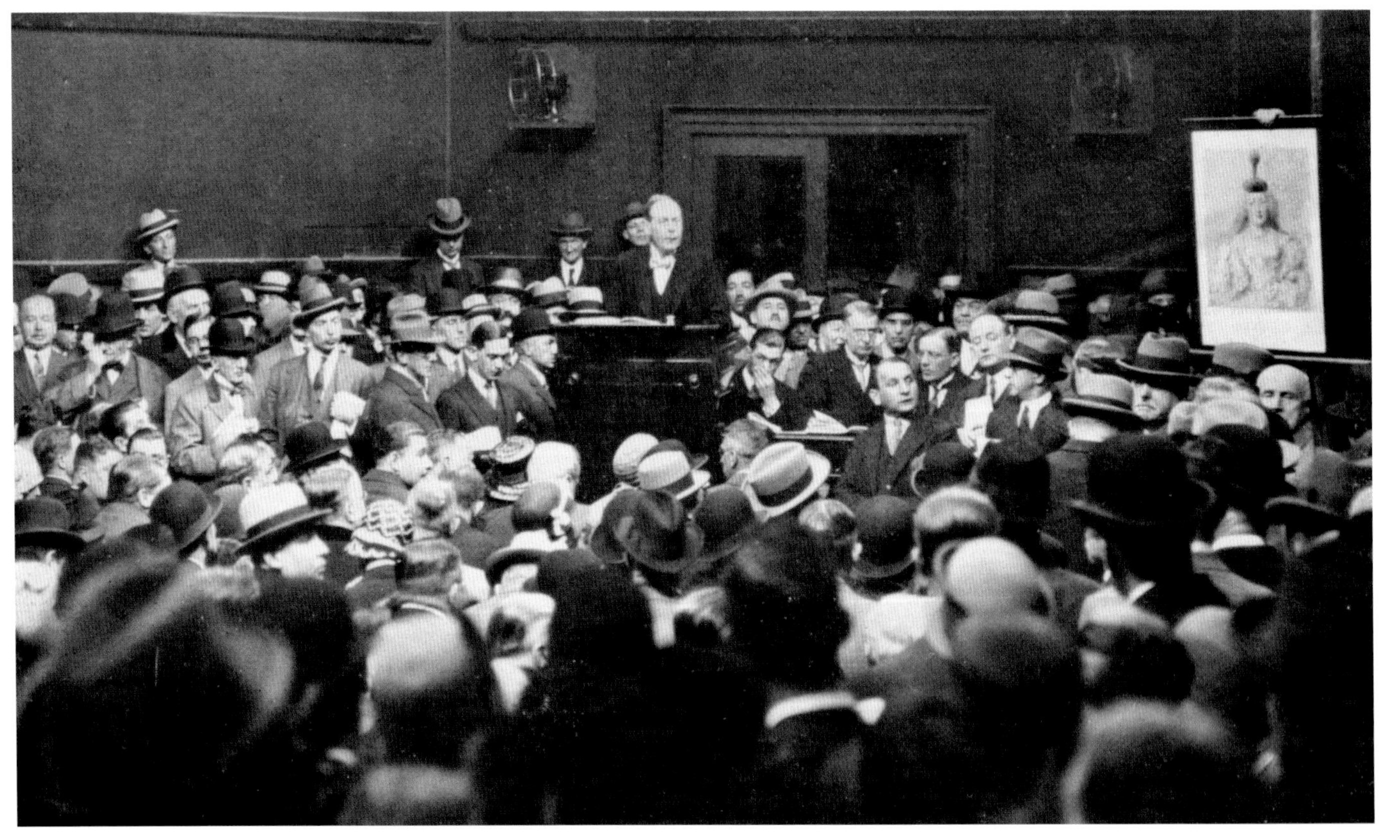

Paolo Veronese, *The Rest on the Flight into Egypt*, c. 1580
This painting was one of the first purchased by John Ringling for his museum.

Diego Velázquez, *Philip IV, King of Spain*, c. 1625
This portrait was acquired at auction by John Ringling in 1928.

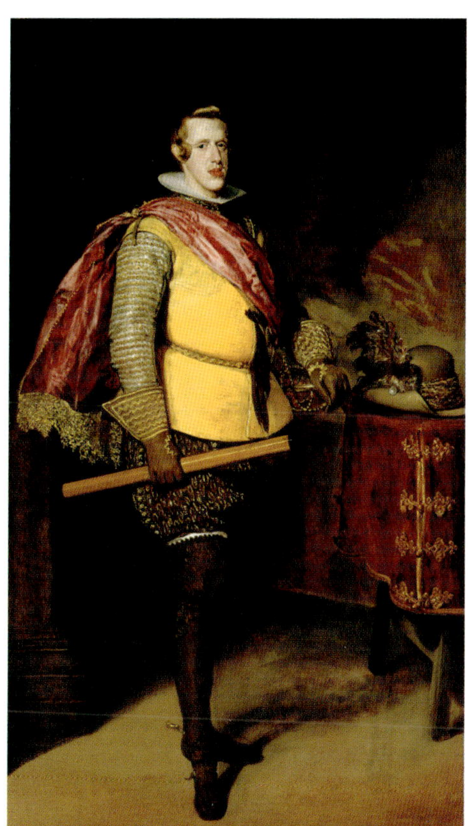

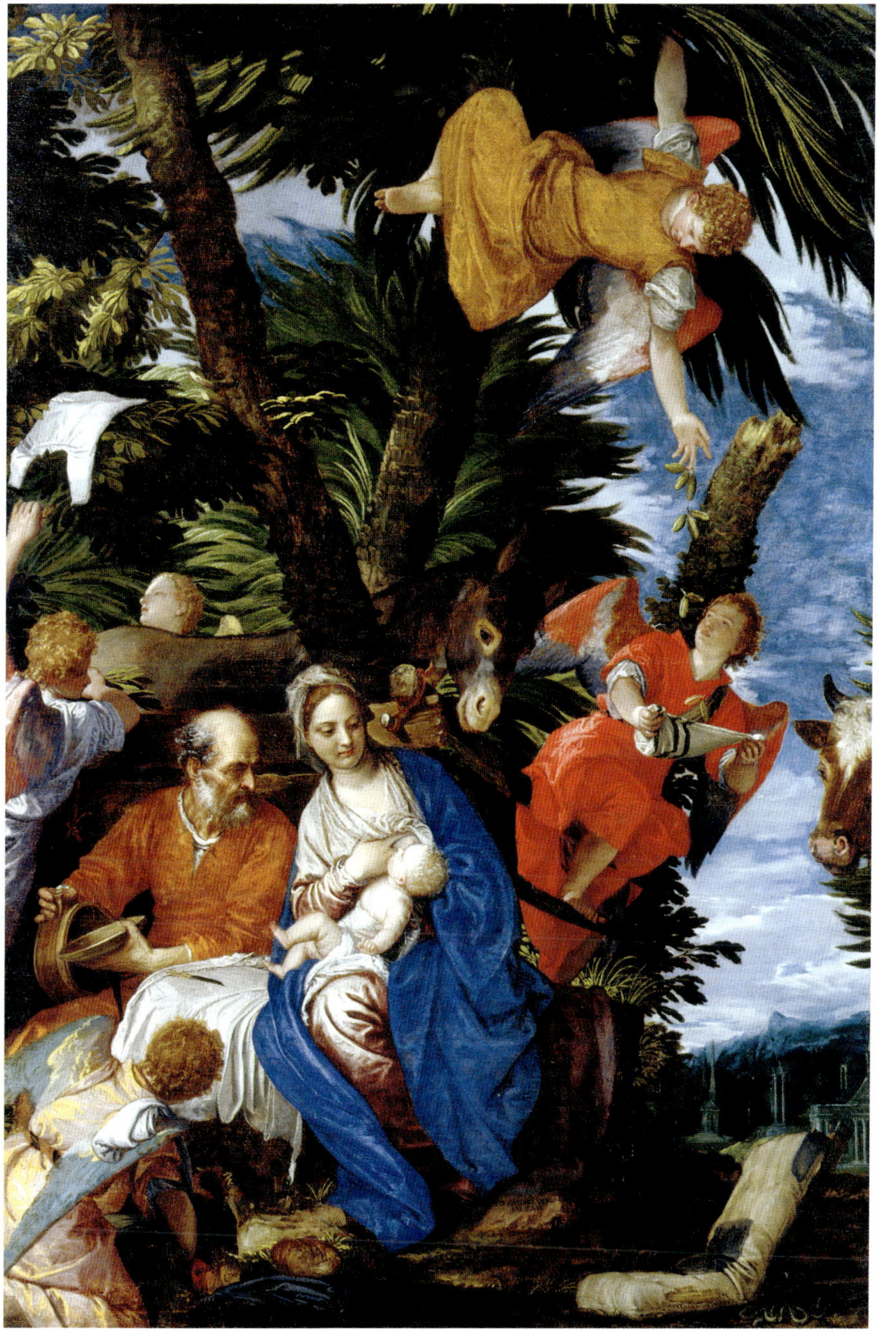

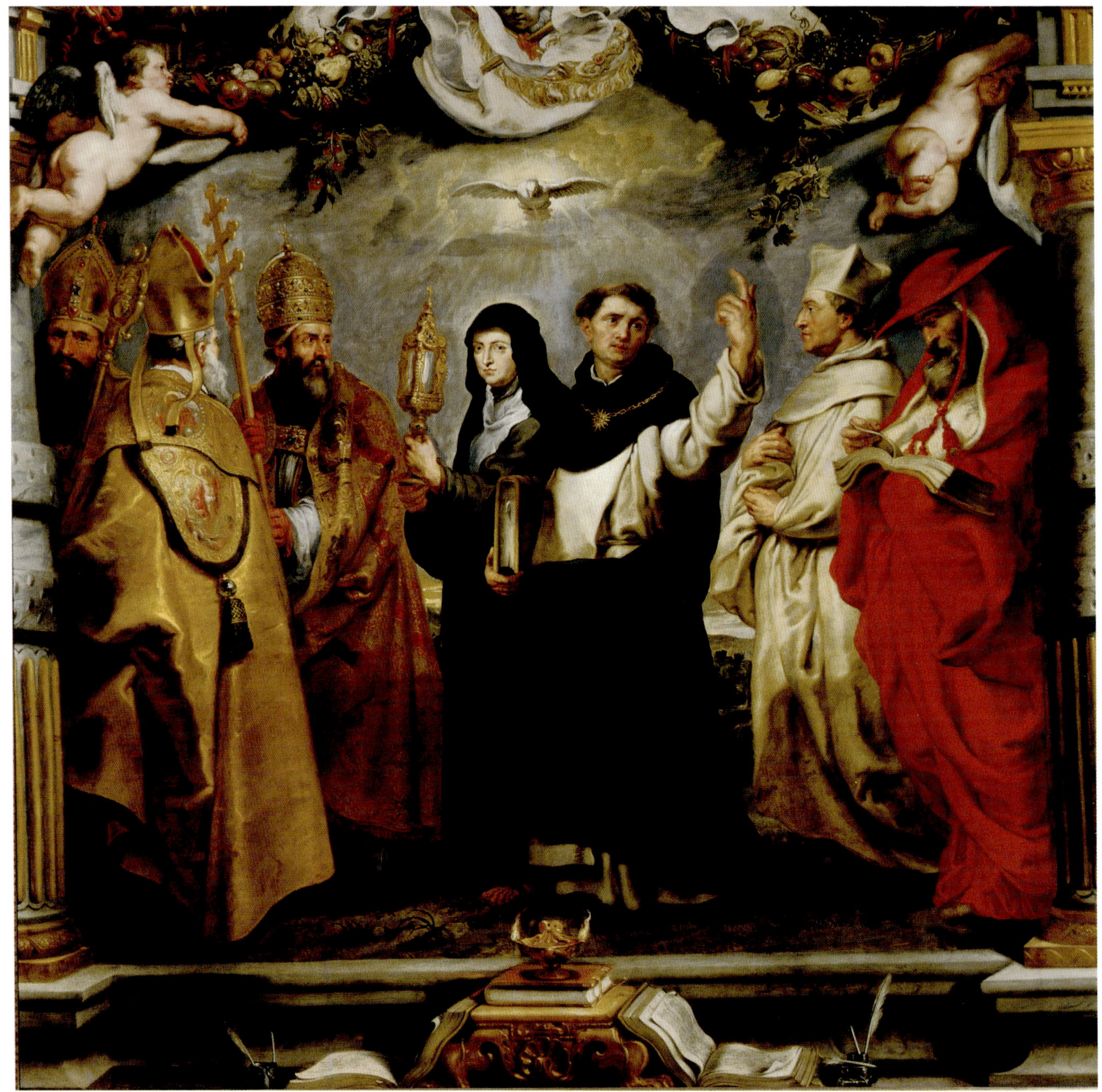

Peter Paul Rubens, *The Defenders of the Eucharist*, c. 1625
This is one of four paintings by artist Peter Paul Rubens purchased by John Ringling in 1926 for $100,000.

Reliquary bust, German, fifteenth century
This bust, purchased by John Ringling from Alva Vanderbilt Belmont, was previously in the possession of dealer Émile Gavet of Paris.

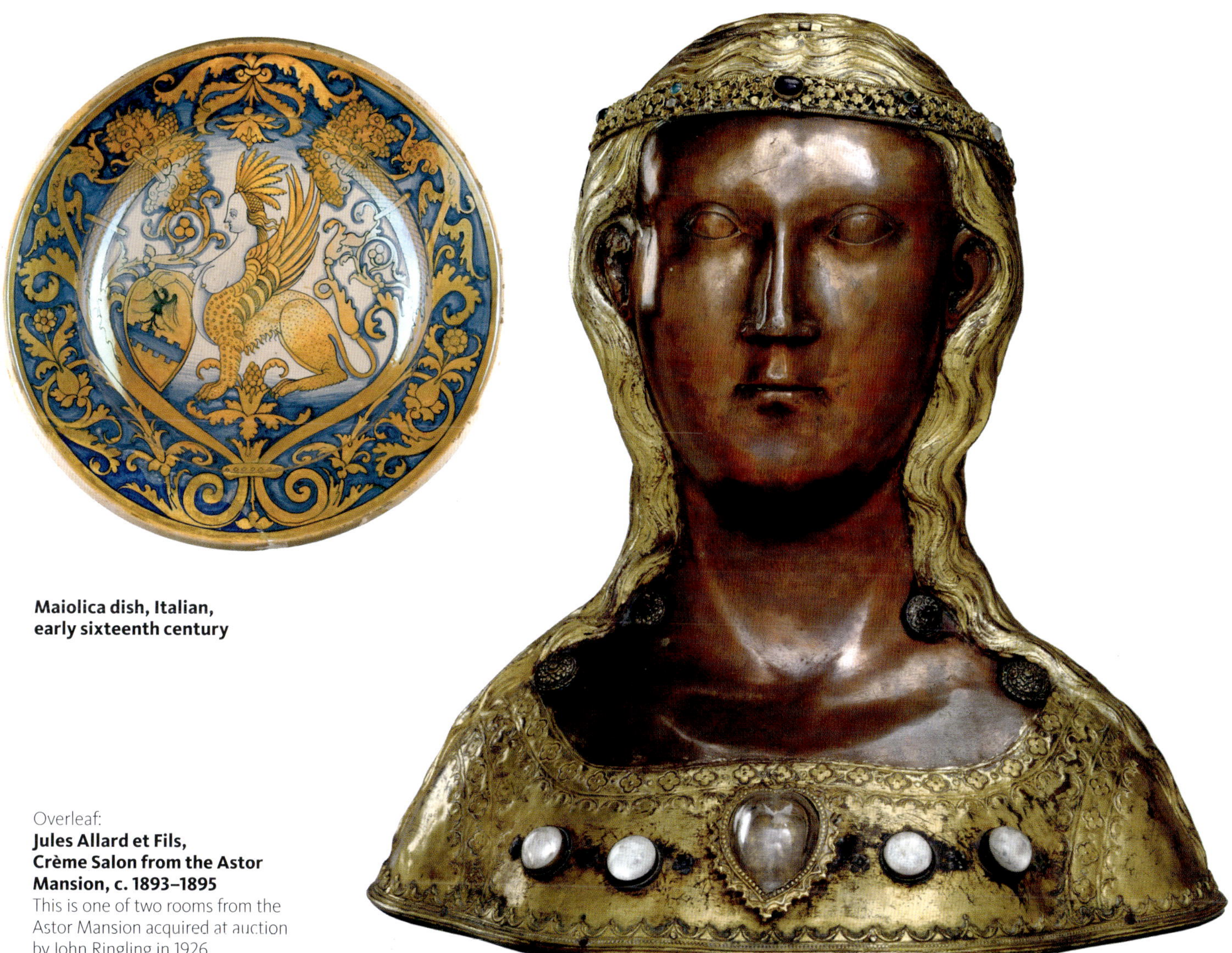

Maiolica dish, Italian, early sixteenth century

Overleaf:
Jules Allard et Fils, Crème Salon from the Astor Mansion, c. 1893–1895
This is one of two rooms from the Astor Mansion acquired at auction by John Ringling in 1926.

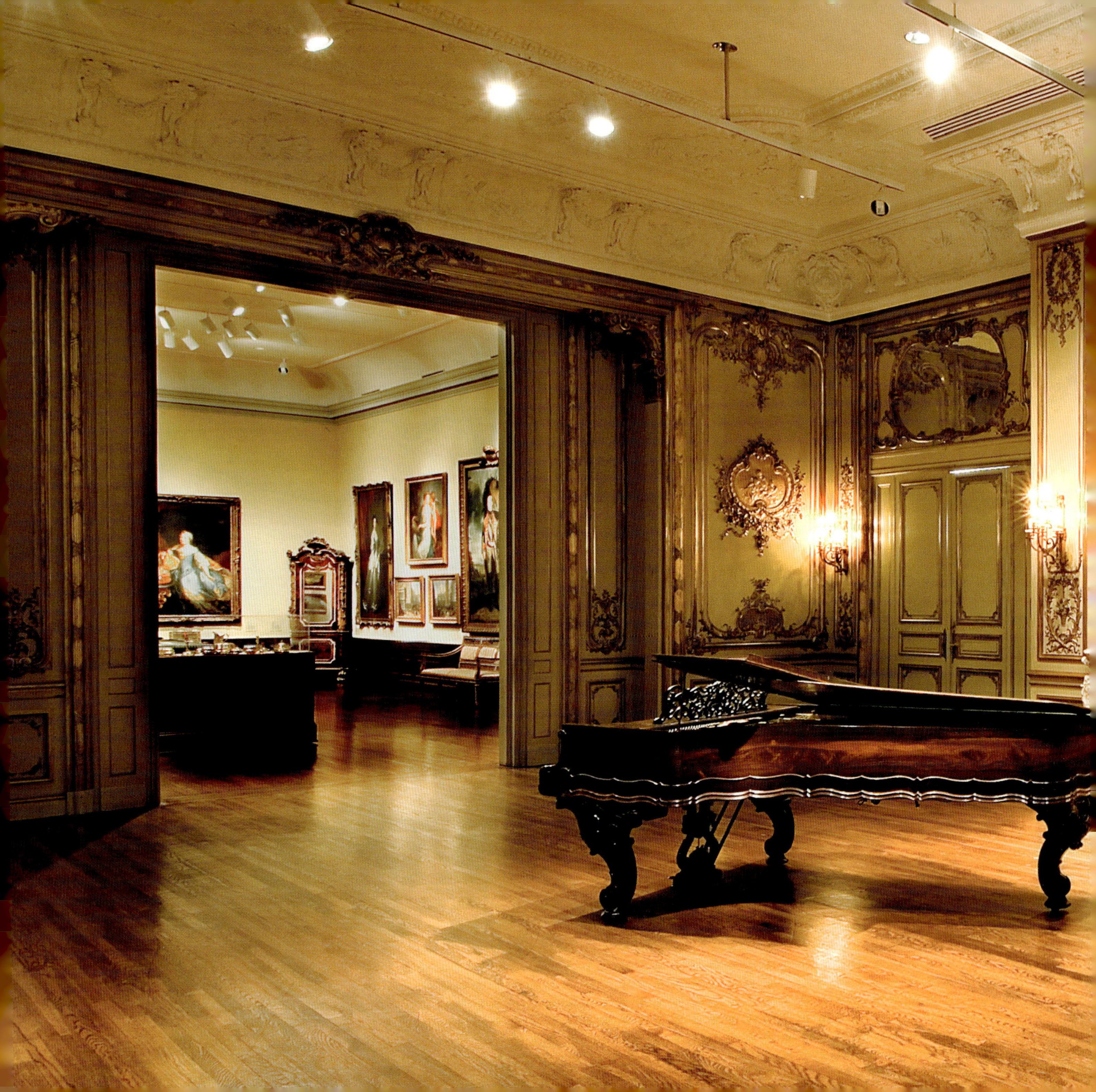

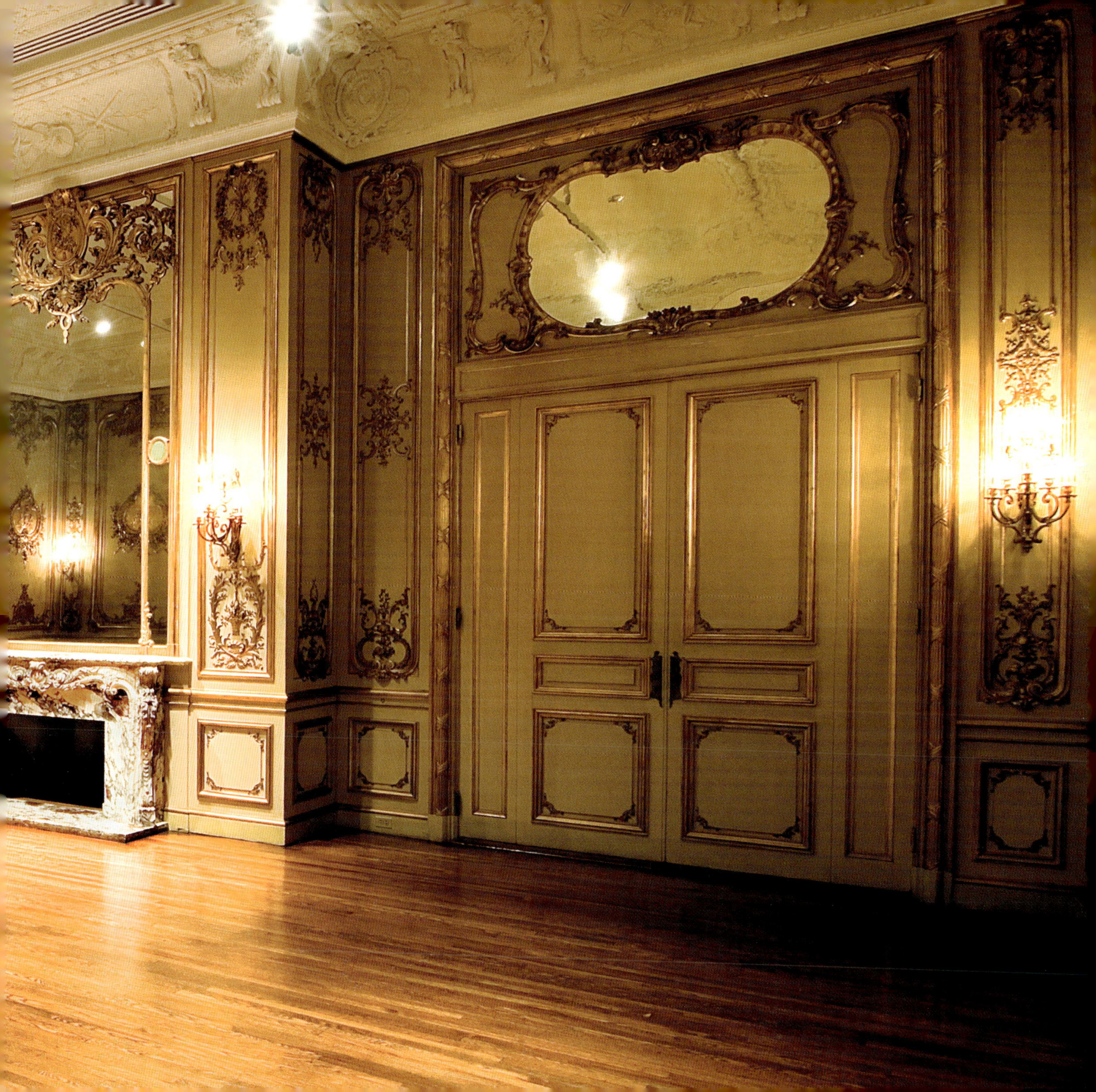

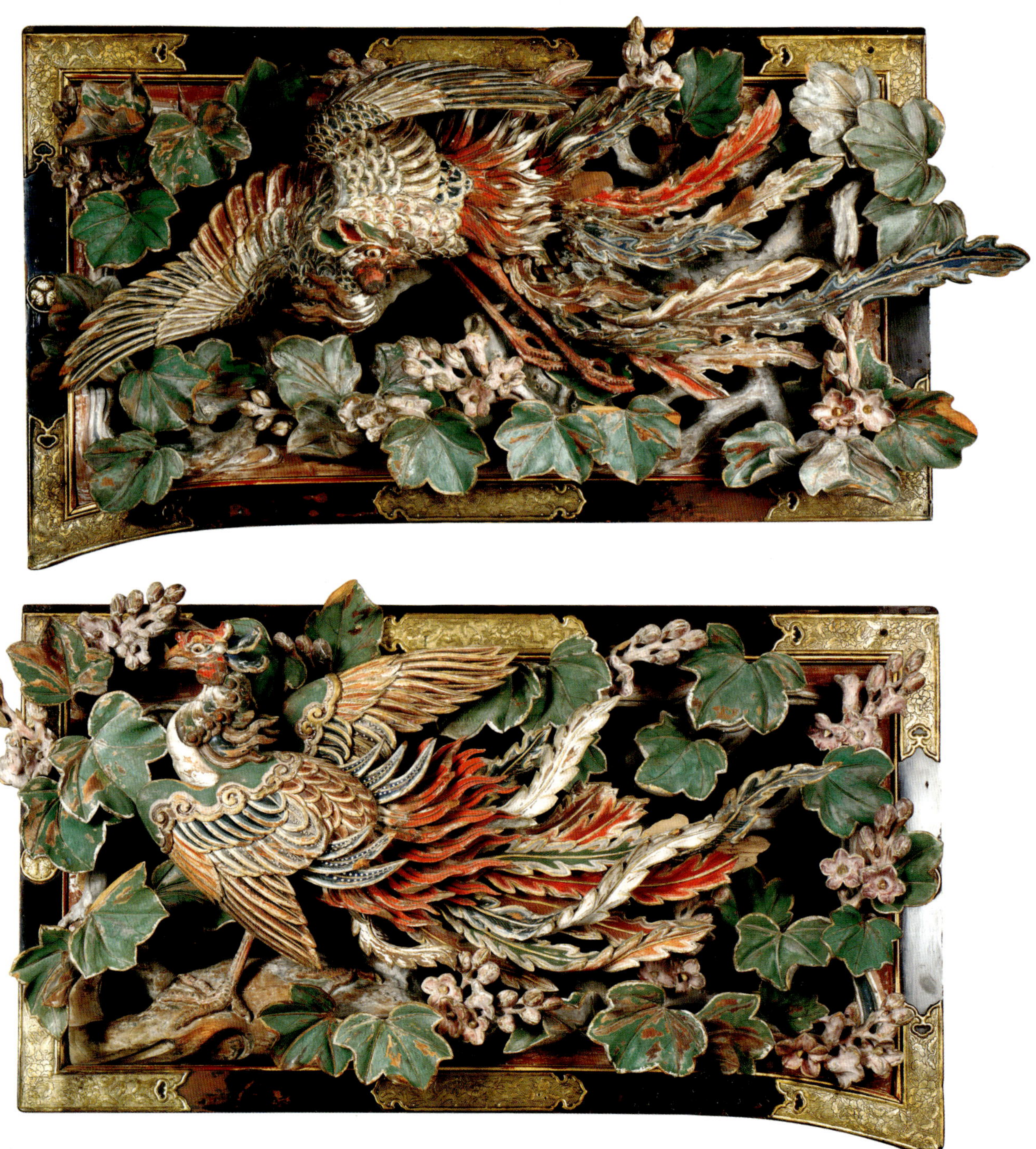

Phoenix panels, Japanese, Meiji period, late nineteenth century
This set of panels, acquired by John Ringling, is similar to one that was exhibited at the World's Columbian Exposition held in Chicago in 1893.

Funerary relief, Cypriot, Classical period, c. 400–300 BC

Storage amphora, Cypriot, Archaic period, c. 750–600 BC
This ancient pot formed part of the collection of Luigi Palma di Cesnola, who was elected the first director of the Metropolitan Museum of Art in 1879.

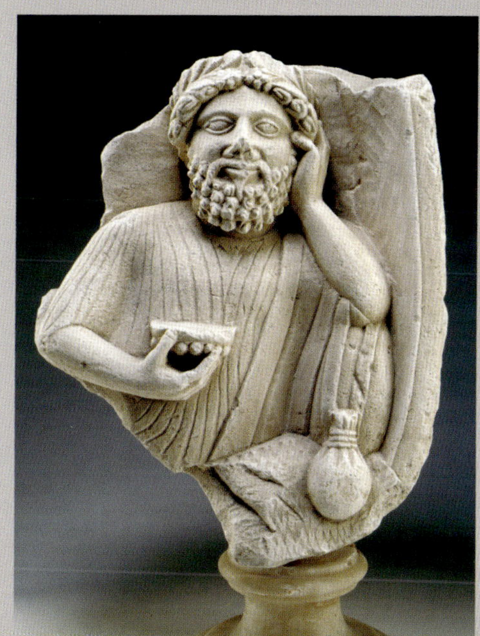

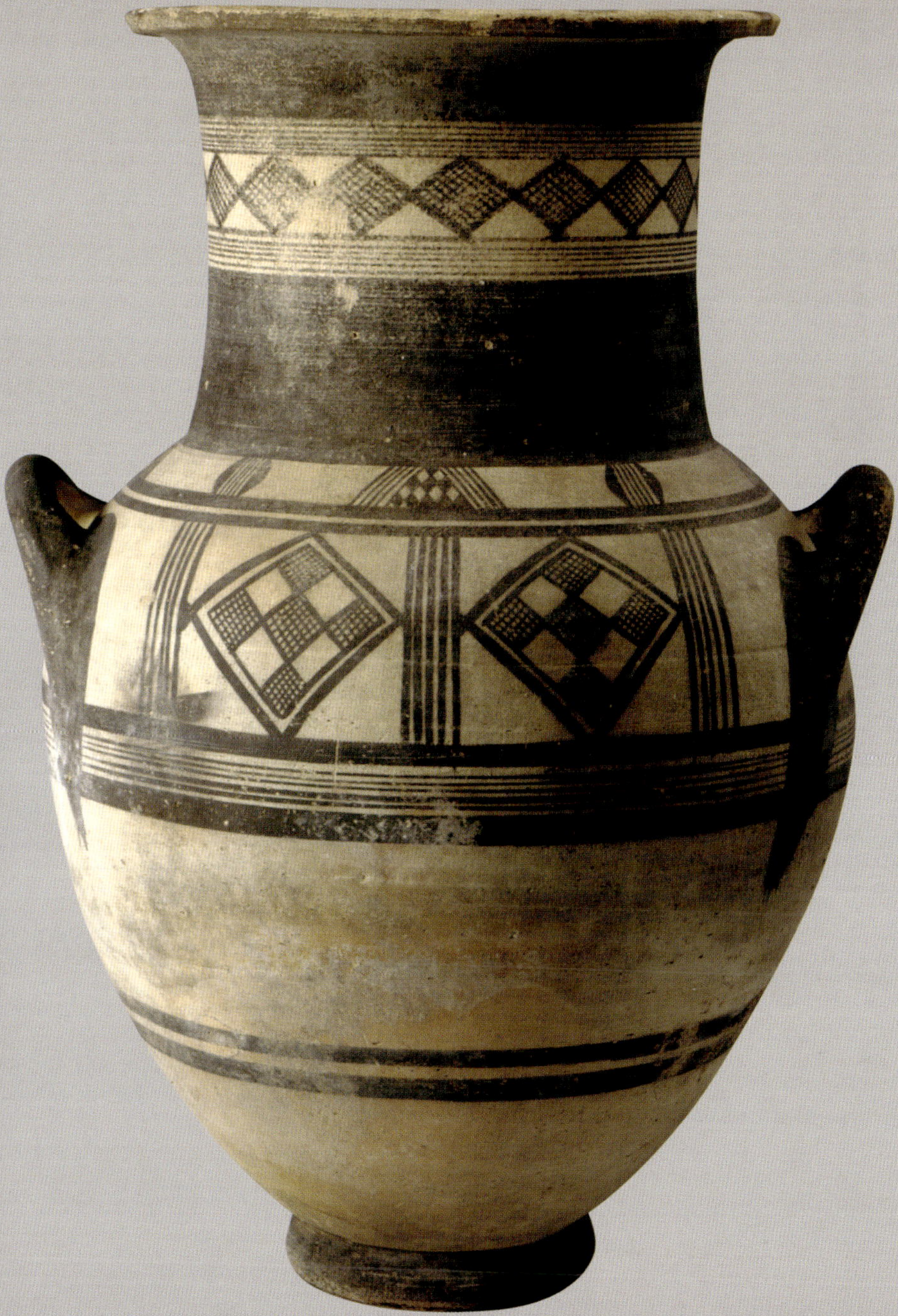

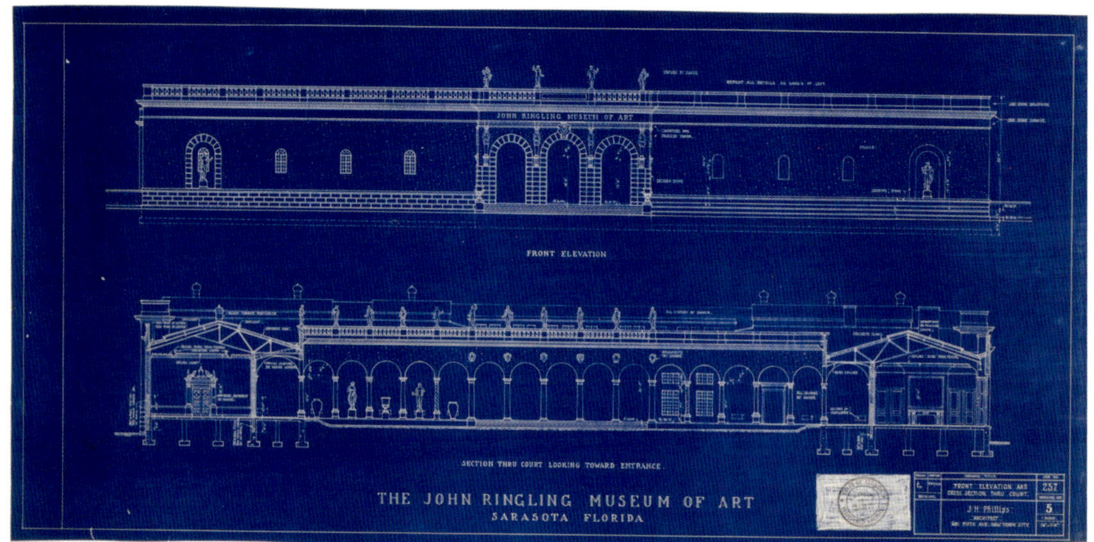

John Phillips, front elevation and cross-section of the Museum of Art, 1926

Museum of Art under construction, c. 1928–1929

Museum of Art, 1940s

previously displayed at Marble House in Newport, Rhode Island. He also added a small selection of works of Asian art and more than 2,000 Cypriot antiquities from the collection of Luigi Palma di Cesnola, formerly owned by the Metropolitan Museum of Art in New York City.

Architect John Phillips designed the Museum of Art in Sarasota to resemble a palace of the Italian Renaissance, considered by John Ringling to be the height of Western civilization. It consisted of a U-shaped structure of twenty-one galleries, with loggias and a courtyard spanned by a bridge.

A patch of swampland to the east of Ca' d'Zan was selected as the site for the museum. Once the land was drained (and the alligators were removed), construction on the museum began in 1928. The museum opened for a single day two years later. It was attended by more than 10,000 visitors, whose number exceeded the population of Sarasota at the time. Crowd control for the event was provided by a group of local Boy Scouts.

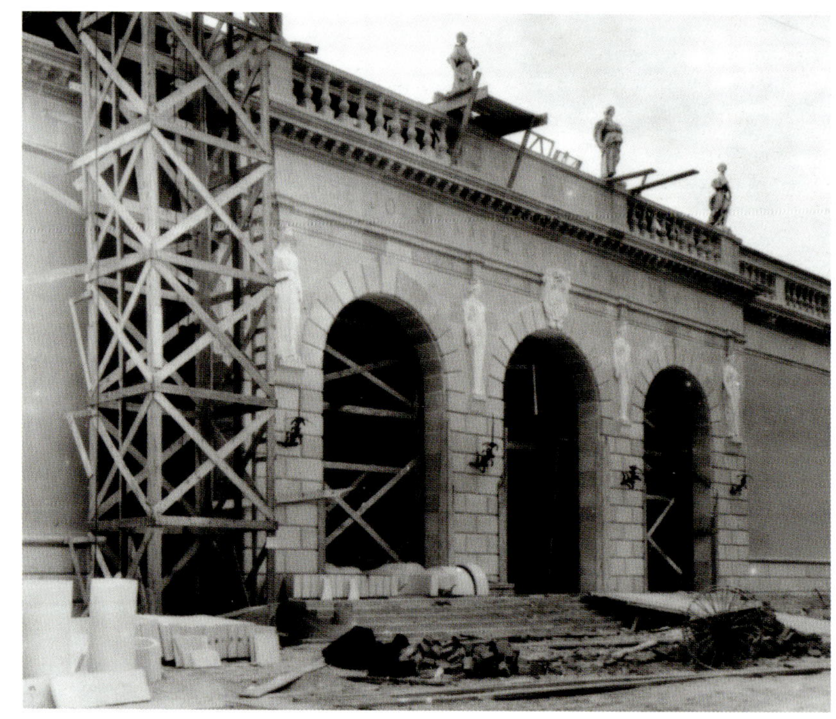

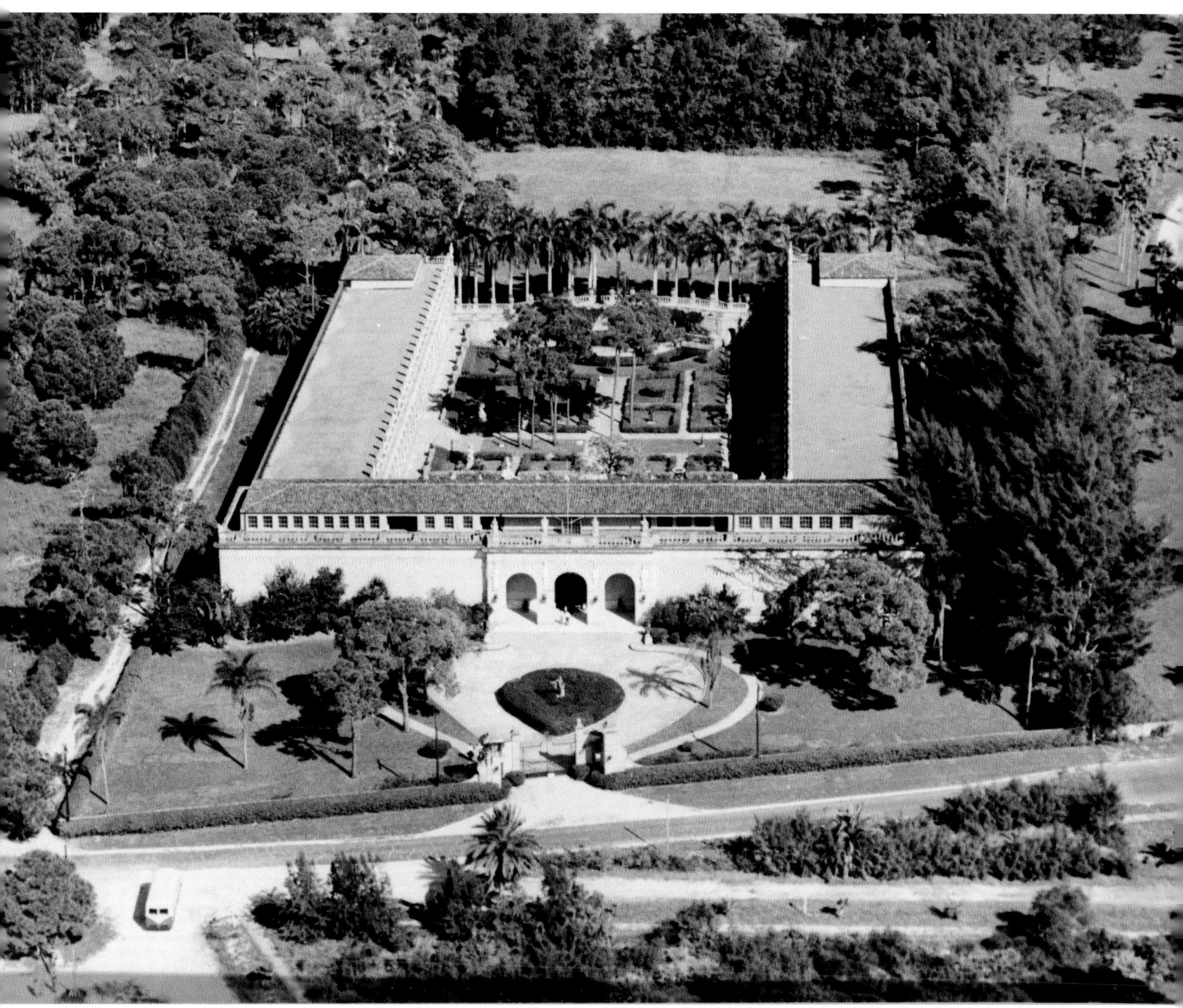

Catalogue from the Chiurazzi Foundry, 1900
The courtyard of the Museum of Art is decorated with copies of Classical and Renaissance sculptures bought by John Ringling from the Chiurazzi Foundry in Naples, Italy.

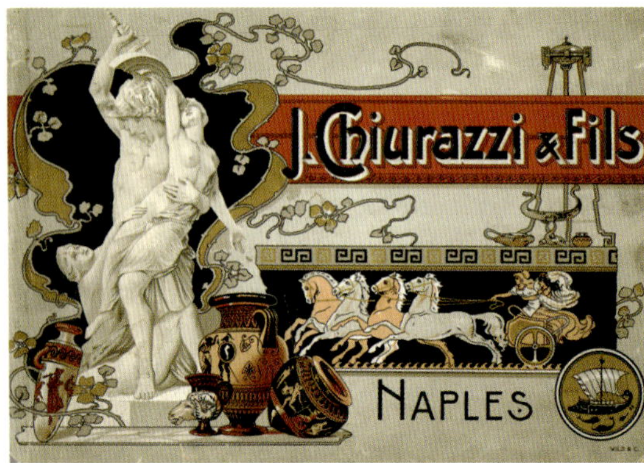

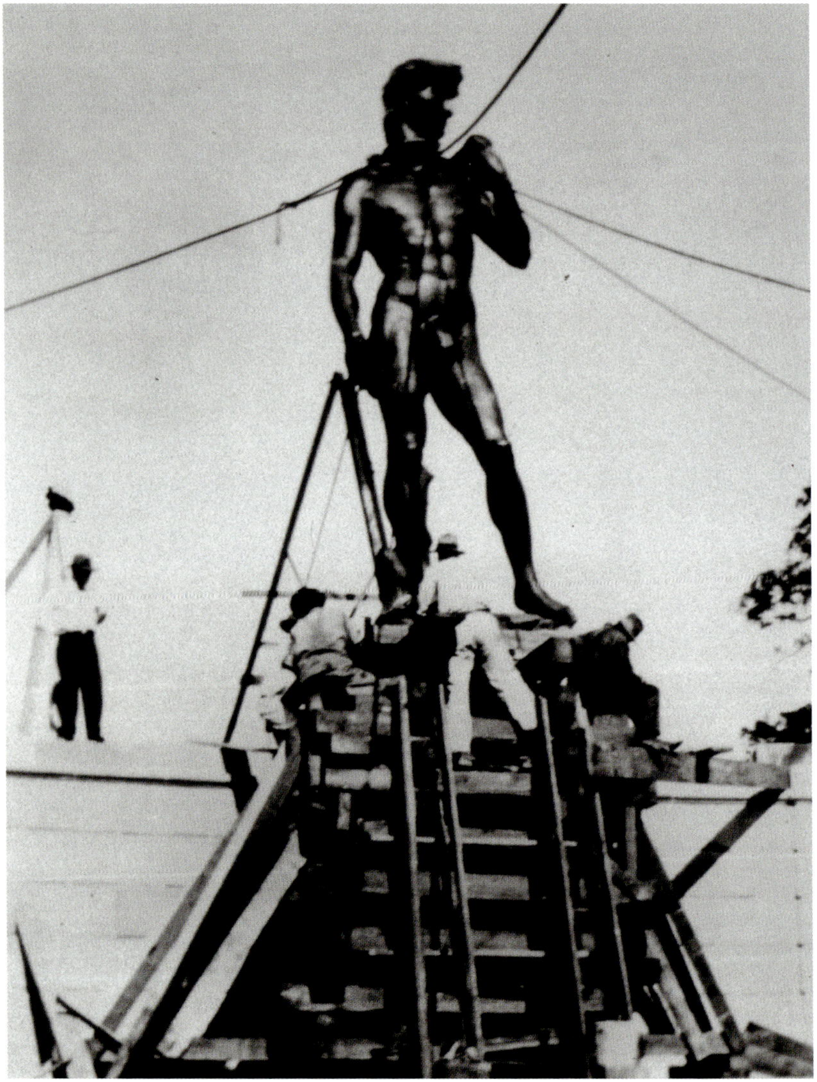

Following a period of closure, in preparation for the publication of a catalogue, the museum reopened permanently in 1932.

Two new wings were added to the museum in 1966 and 2007. The latter, known as the Searing Wing, houses a series of galleries used for special exhibitions and rotating displays of modern and contemporary art, including photographs and other works on paper. The galleries surround a courtyard with a Skyspace by artist James Turrell.

The collection continues to grow through gifts and purchases, particularly of Asian, modern, and contemporary art. A center for Asian art, combining part of the 1966 wing with a new pavilion, designed by the architectural firm of Machado and Silvetti Associates, is scheduled to open in 2015. It will consist of Asian art galleries, storage and study rooms, and a lecture theater with views of the grounds and bay.

Statue of *David* being installed, c. 1929
This copy of the statue of *David* by artist Michelangelo Buonarroti has become a symbol of Sarasota.

James Turrell,
***Joseph's Coat*, 2011**
This Skyspace is an architectural installation in which viewers experience the ever-changing sky.

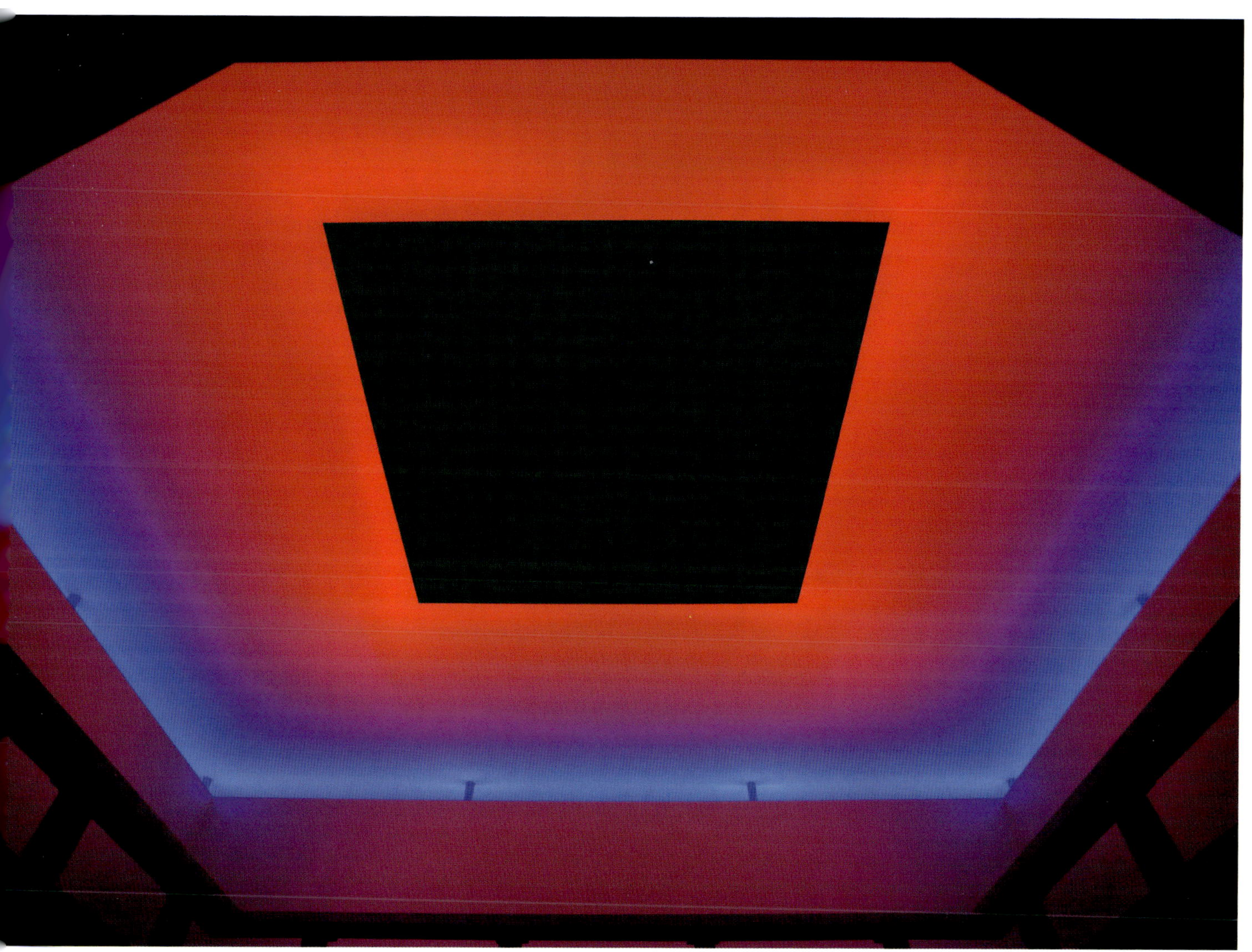

Syd Solomon,
***Silent World*, 1961**
Artist Syd Solomon lived in Sarasota and taught at The Ringling early in his career.

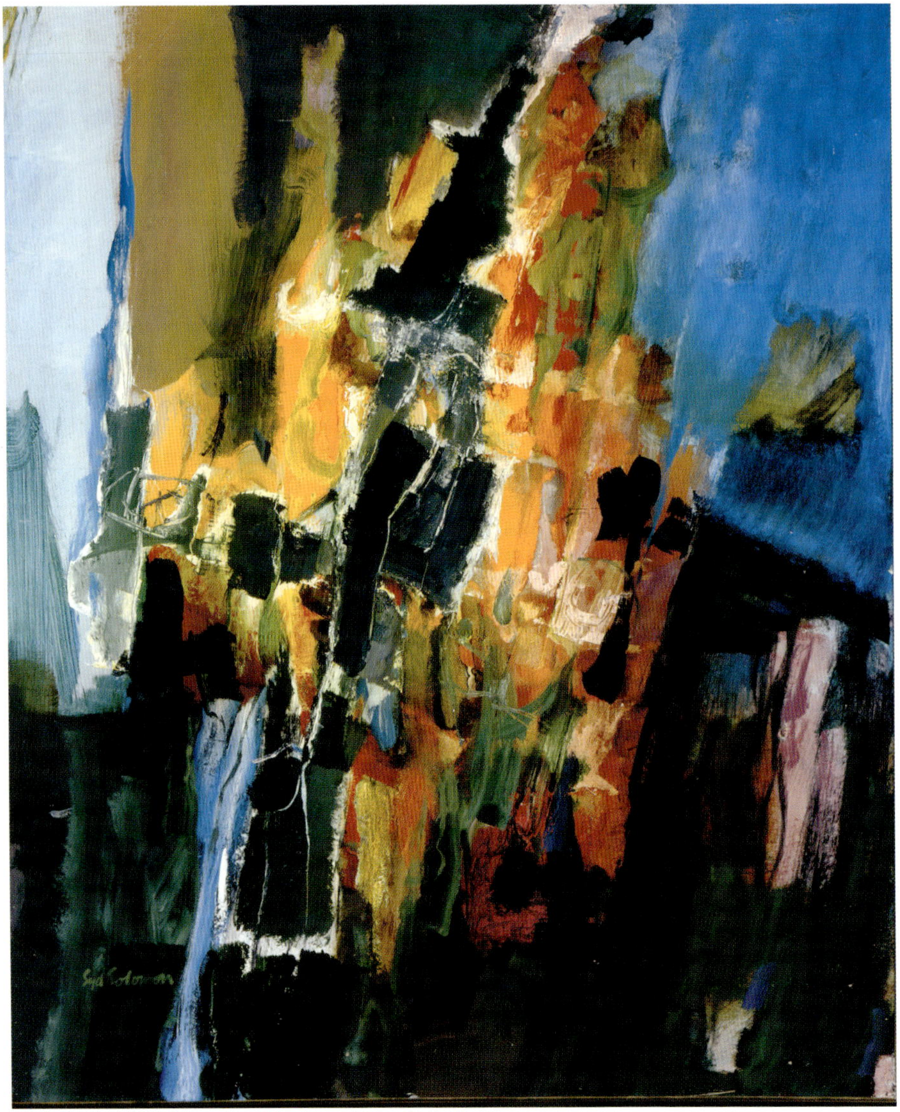

R. Luke DuBois, *Circus Sarasota: Dolly Jacobs*, 2014
This is one of a series of five video portraits of contemporary circus performers commissioned by The Ringling in 2014.

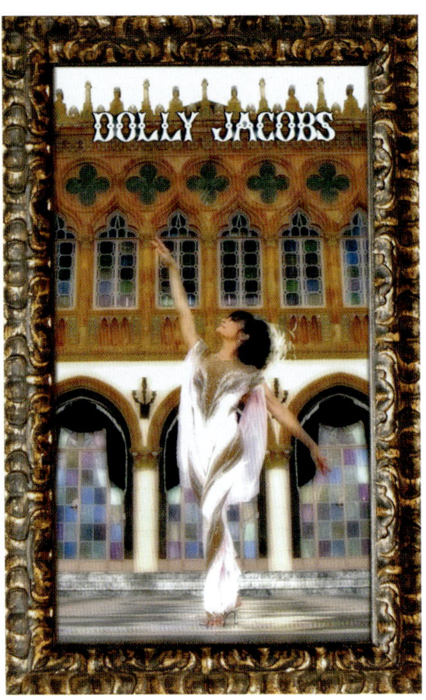

RINGLING COLLEGE OF ART AND DESIGN

John Ringling planned to build an art school adjoining the Museum of Art, where young artists would learn from, and be inspired by, the works in his collection. He hoped that the combination of a school and museum would attract established artists to the local community and, in time, give rise to a "Sarasota School" of painting.

While lack of funds forced John to reject this idea, he did support the establishment of an art school in a vacant hotel nearby in 1931. Originally affiliated with Southern College of Lakeland, the school became an independent entity two years later. It has since developed into Ringling College of Art and Design, one of the leading institutions of its type in the nation.

John Phillips, aerial view of the Museum of Art, 1928
This view shows the proposed art school that was never built.

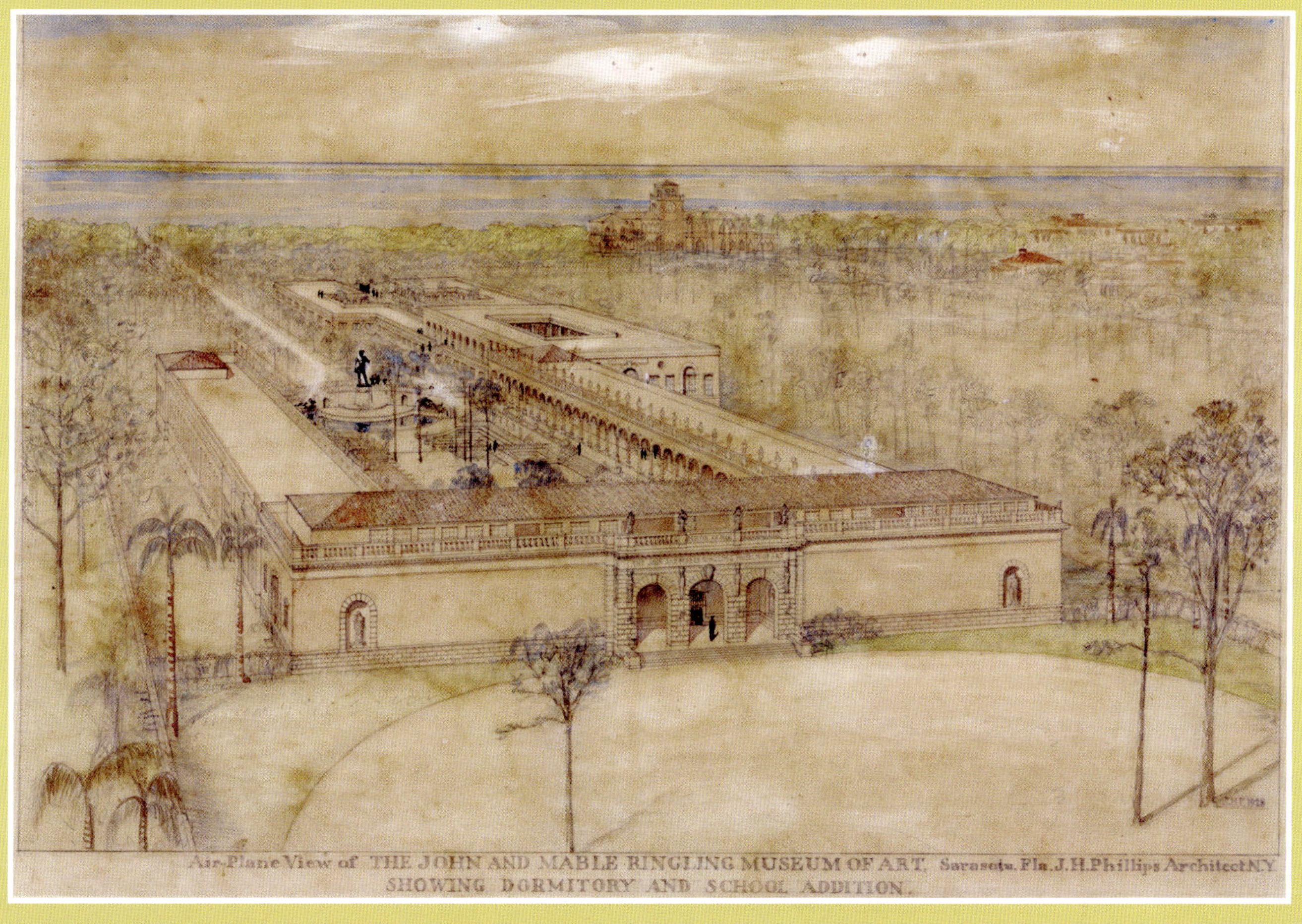

CIRCUS MUSEUM

Chick Austin established the Circus Museum in 1948 to honor the memory of John Ringling. It was the first museum in the country to document the rich history of the American circus.

The museum occupies a former garage where the Ringlings parked their Rolls Royces and Pierce-Arrows. Austin added a large rotunda resembling a circus tent and decorated the

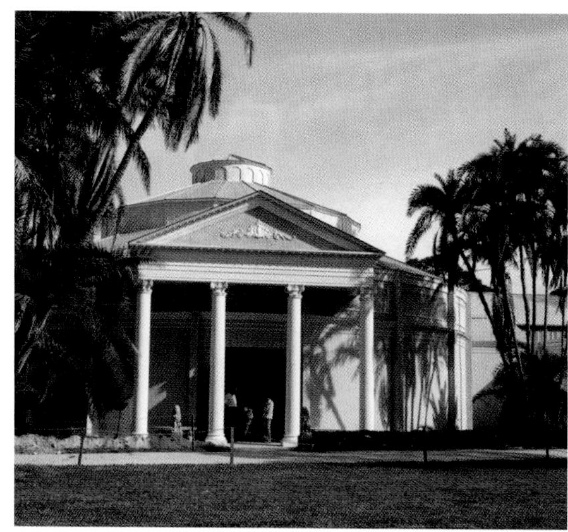

Circus Museum, c. 1972

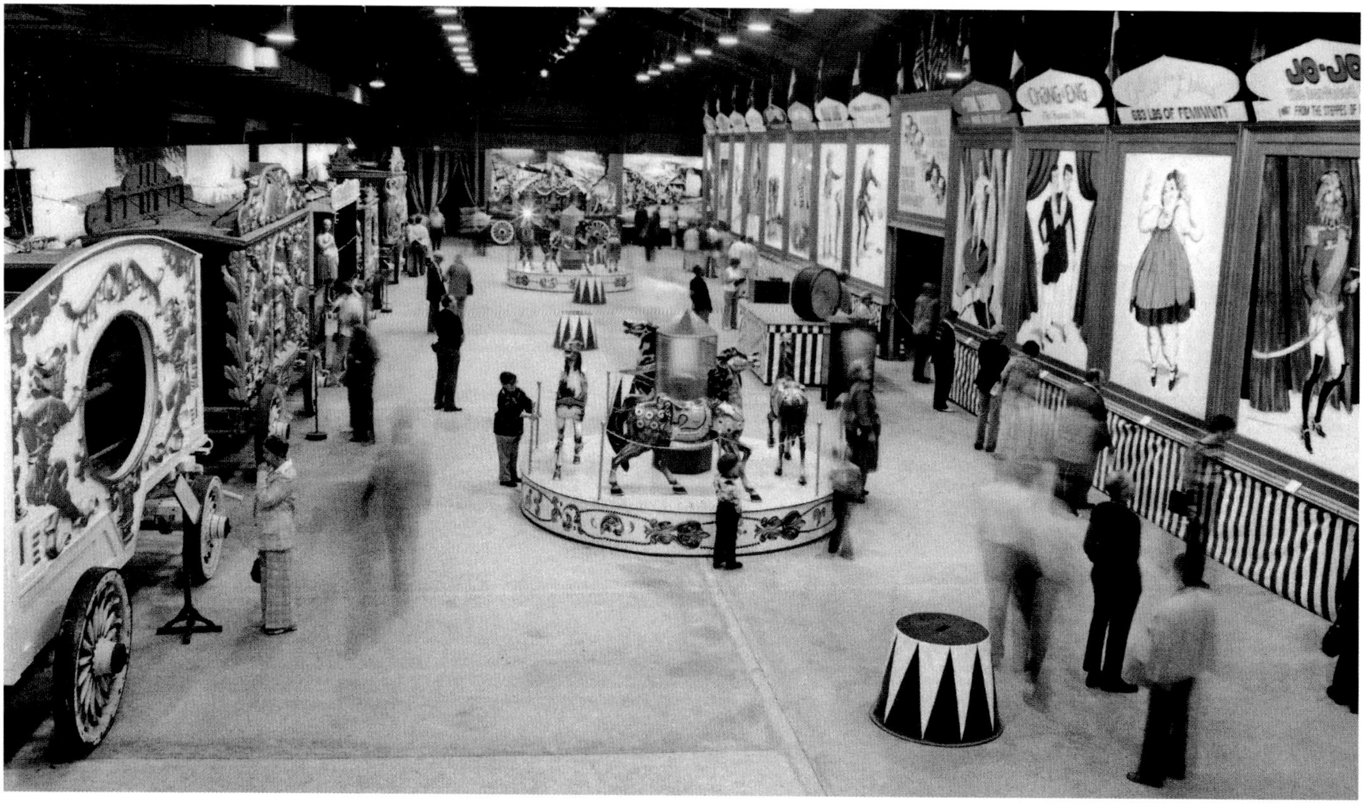

Wagon room of the Circus Museum, c. 1975

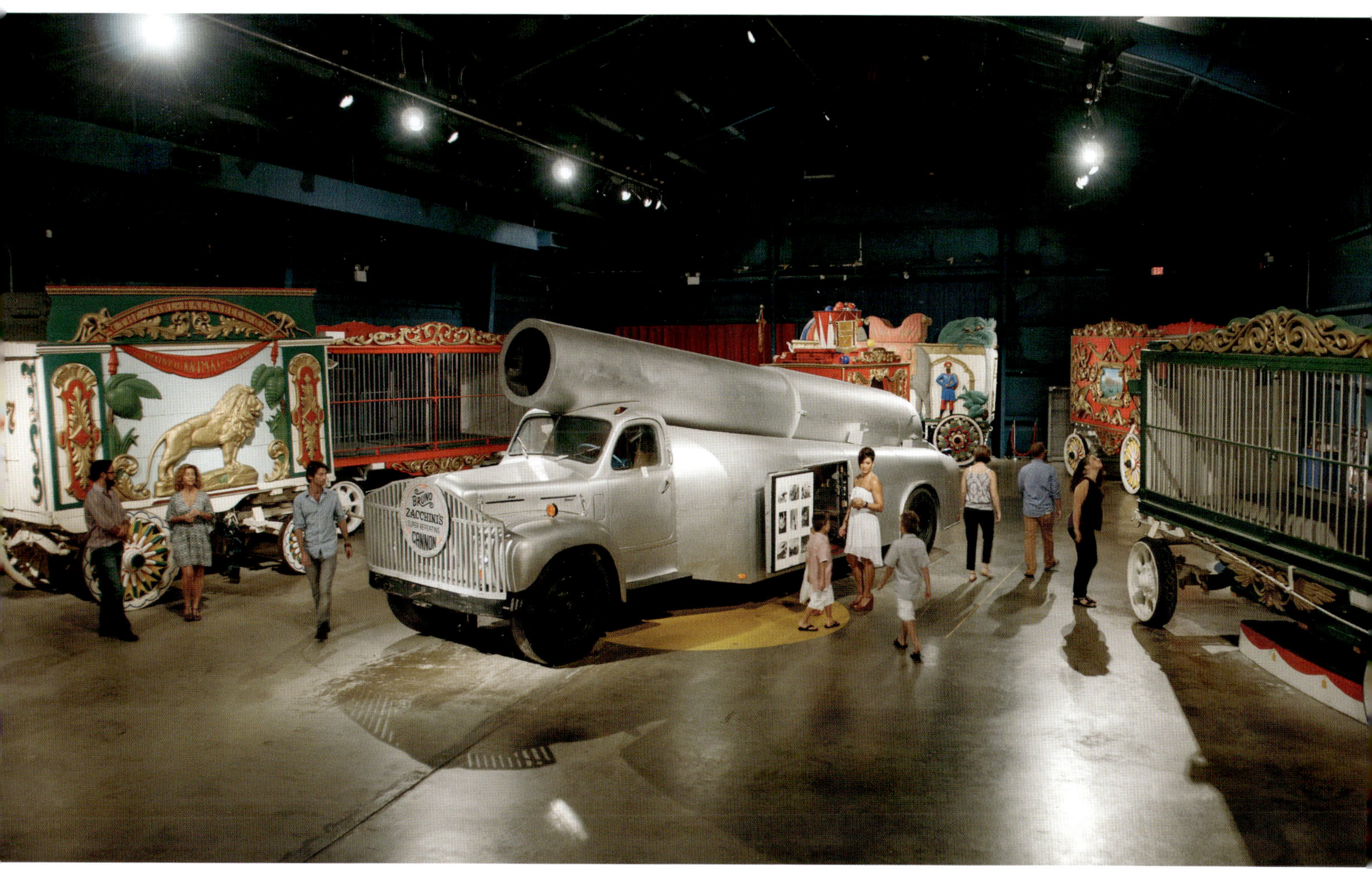

Wagon room of the Circus Museum today

interior with architectural elements from one of the Astor residences. This gave the museum a sense of drama that appealed to Austin, who had a passion for theater.

The collection originally consisted of costumes and props donated by local circus families. Other artifacts, such as wagons and equipment, entered the collection after the closure of the circus winter quarters in Sarasota in 1959. Exhibition and storage space was added to accommodate this material, some of which was used to recreate a circus backyard, where performers prepared for the show.

A new chapter in the history of the museum began with the opening of the Tibbals Learning Center in 2006. The center houses the Howard Bros. Circus Model, the largest miniature circus in the world, and a timeline of circus history, from antiquity to today. An extension, opened in 2012, features displays on circus performers,

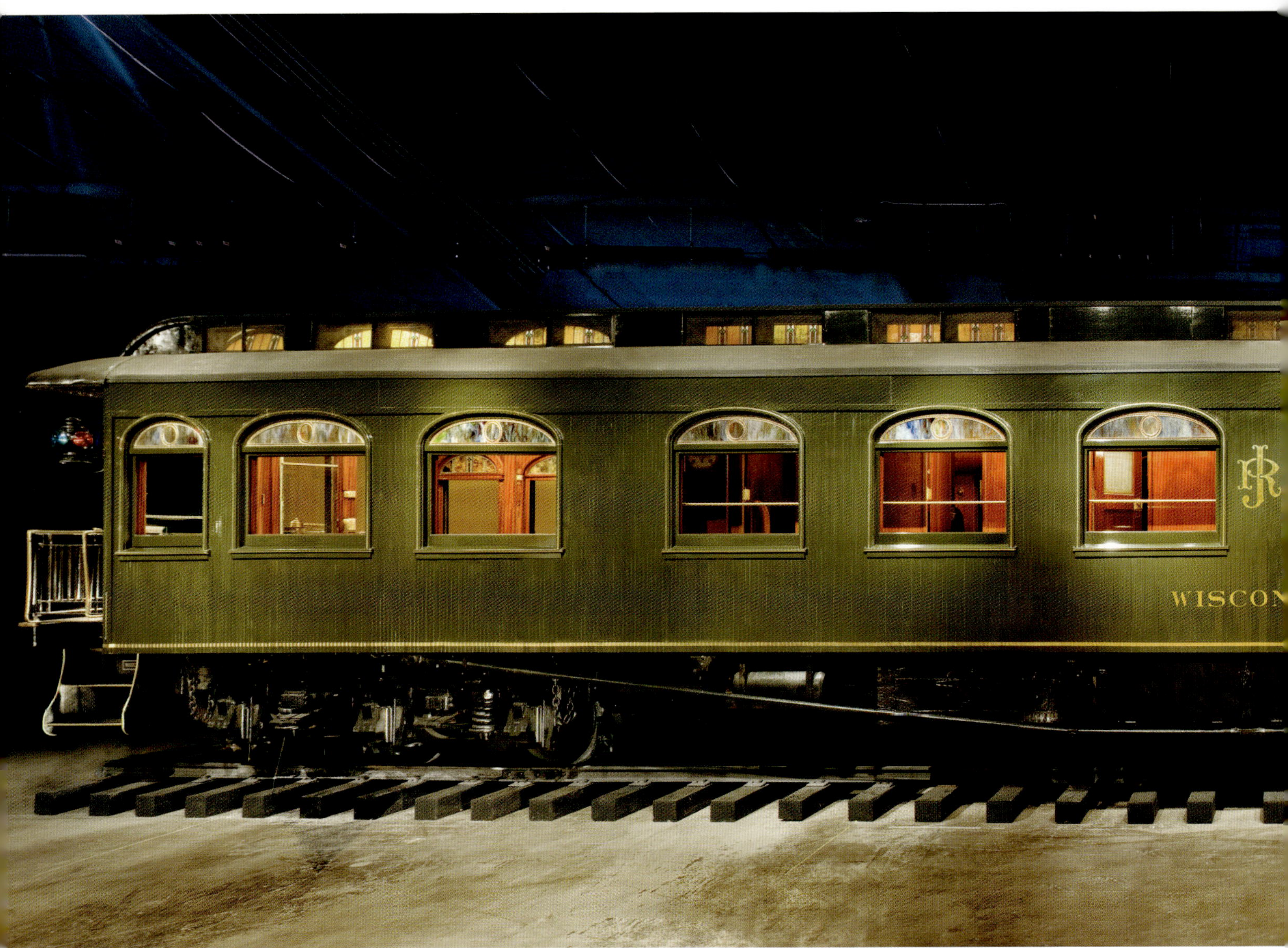

***Wisconsin* railcar, 1905**
John and Mable Ringling used this luxurious private railcar to travel the country for business and pleasure.

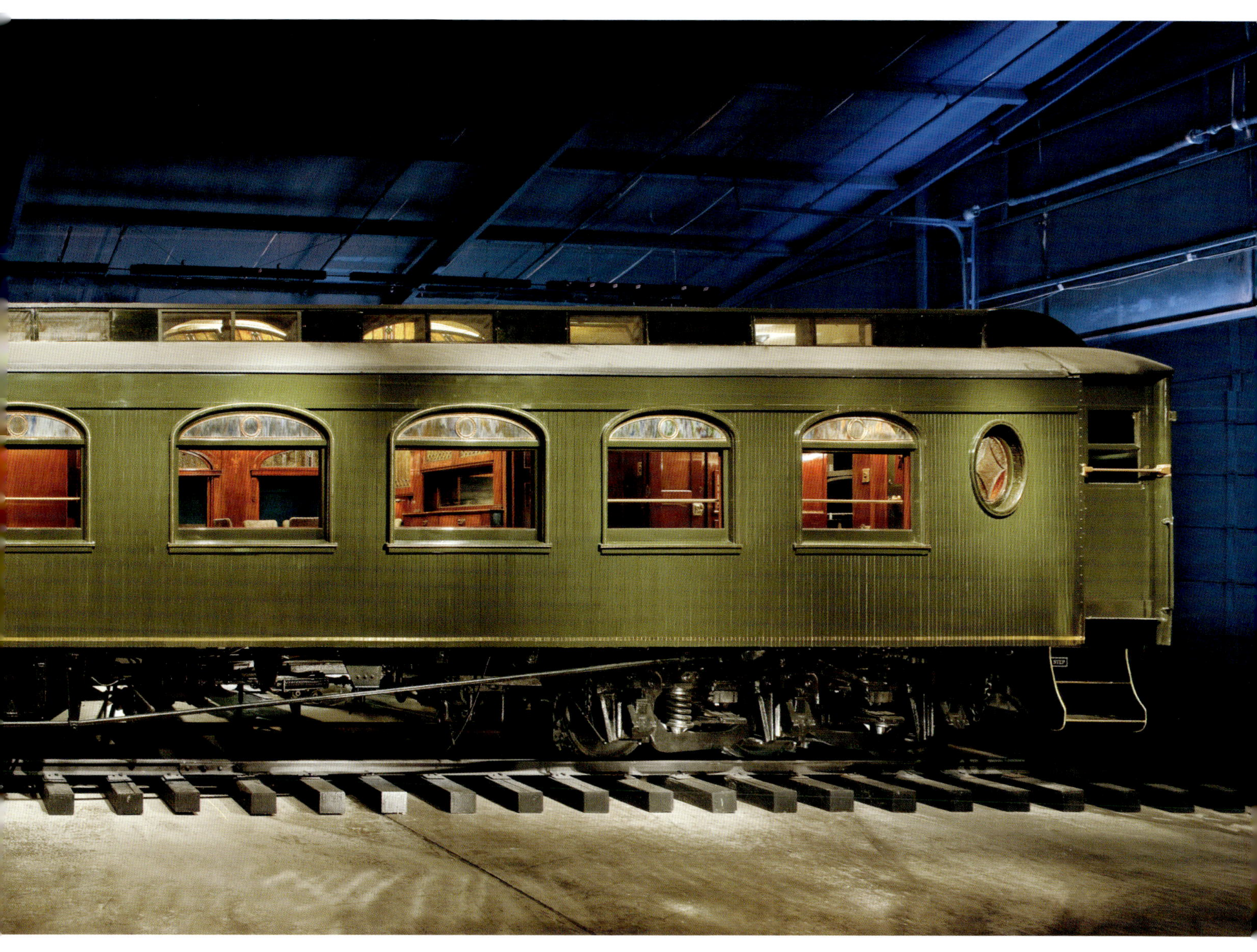

Tibbals Learning Center
The entrance to the center is covered by a tent similar to one used by the Ringling Bros. and Barnum & Bailey Circus in the early twentieth century.

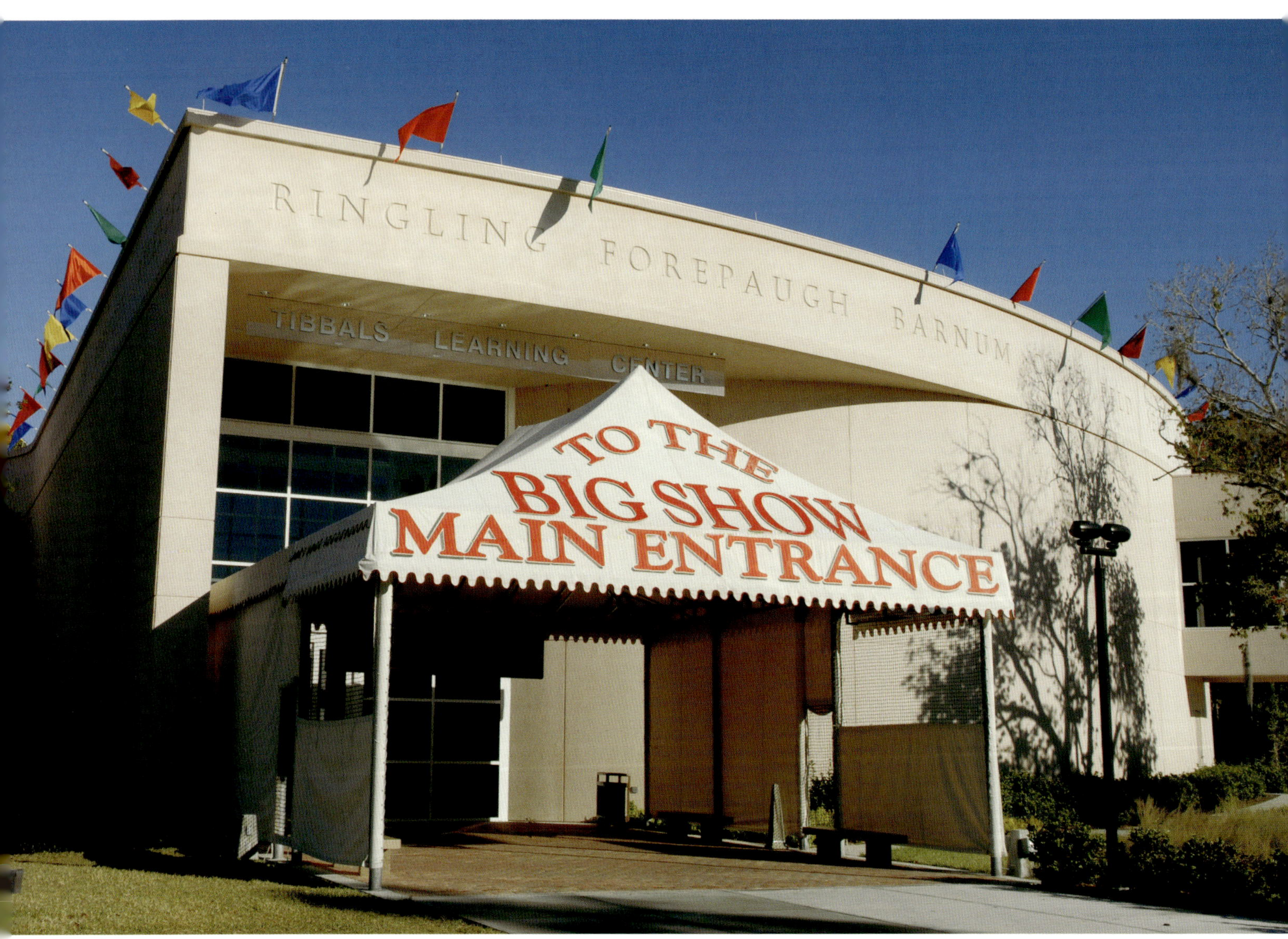

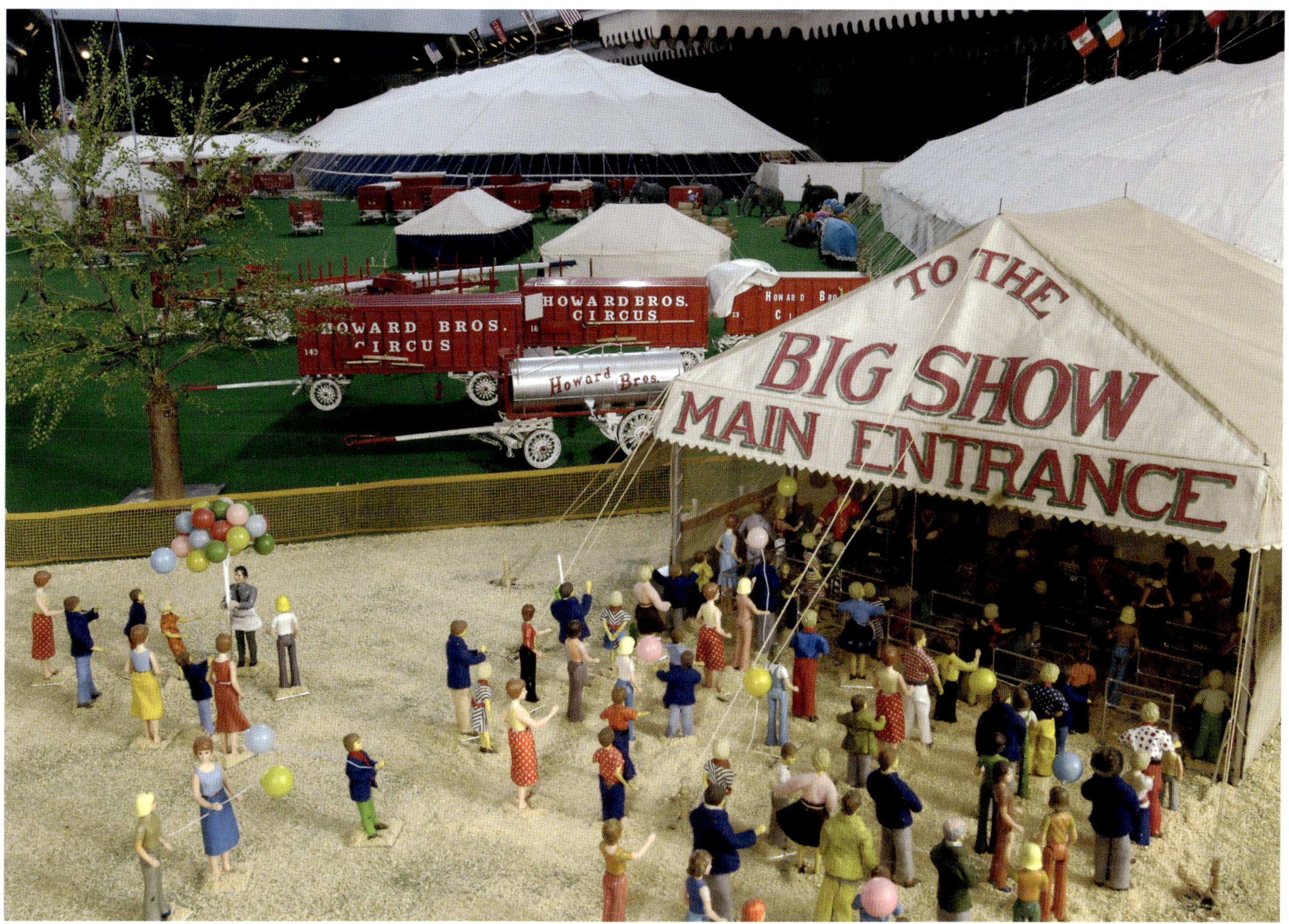

Howard Bros. Circus Model
This model is a ¾ -inch scale replica of the Ringling Bros. and Barnum & Bailey Circus of 1919 to 1938. It is the life's work of Howard Tibbals, who began constructing it in 1956.

past and present, and hands-on interactives that allow visitors of all ages to become center-ring stars.

Behind the scenes of the center is The Ringling Archives. This state-of-the-art facility contains a wealth of material, such as Ringling family papers, institutional records, and circus documents, including posters, programs, and photographs. It is open to researchers by appointment.

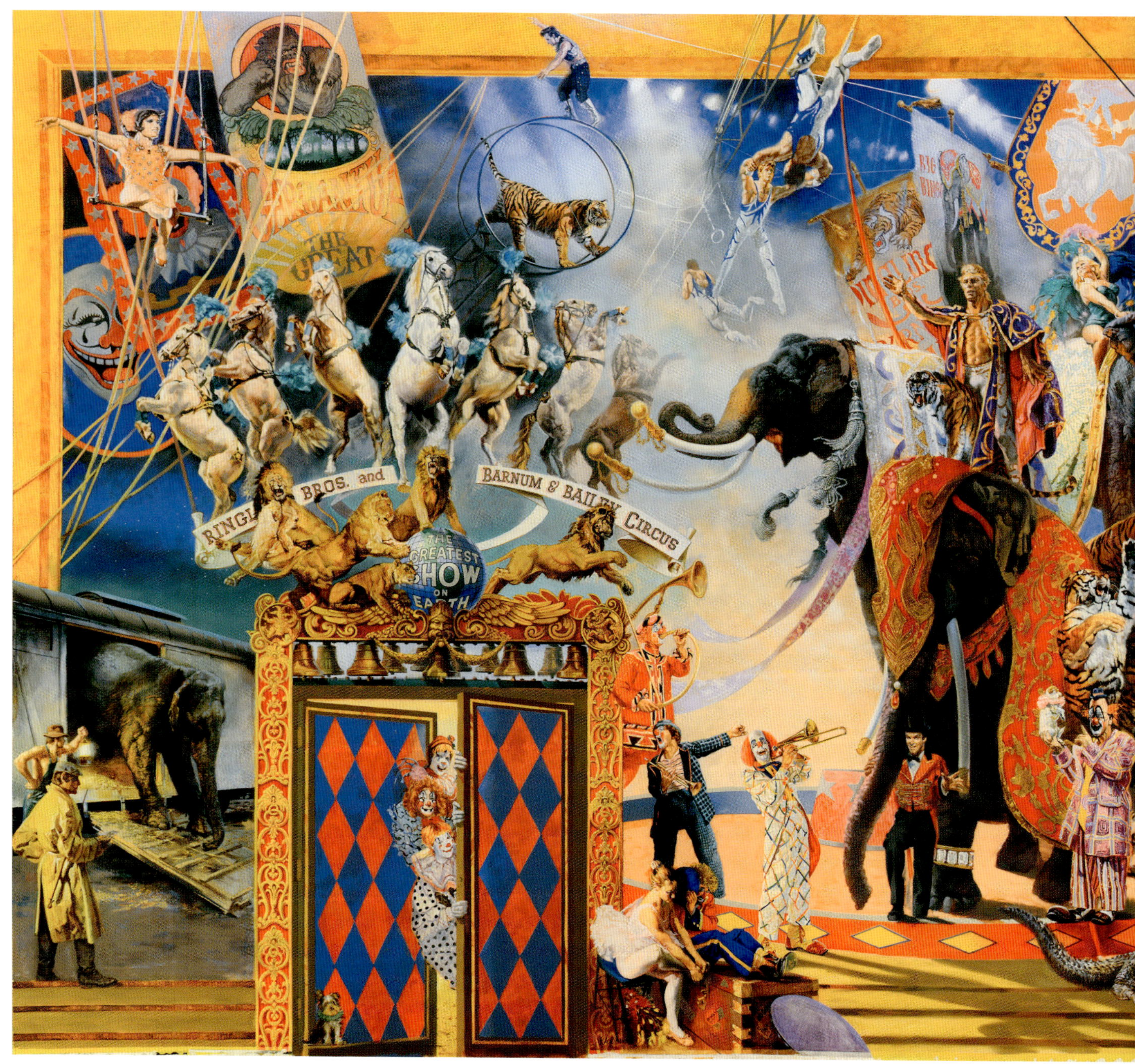
THE GREAT
BROS. and
BARNUM & BAIL
CIRCUS
THE GREATEST SHOW ON EARTH

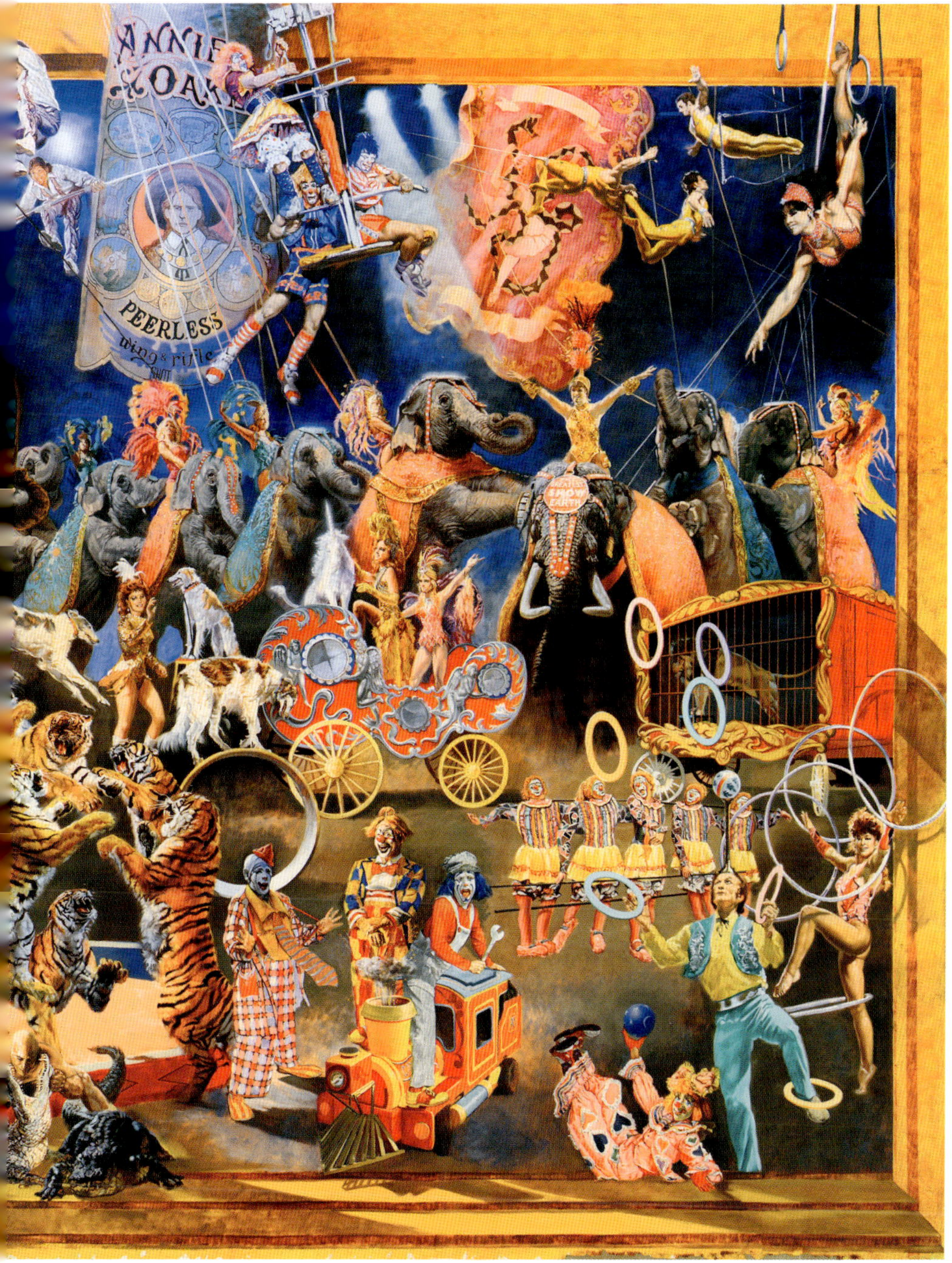

William Woodward, *The Greatest Show on Earth*, 1990
This giant mural originally adorned the lobby of the corporate offices of Feld Entertainment, the parent company of the Ringling Bros. and Barnum & Bailey Circus.

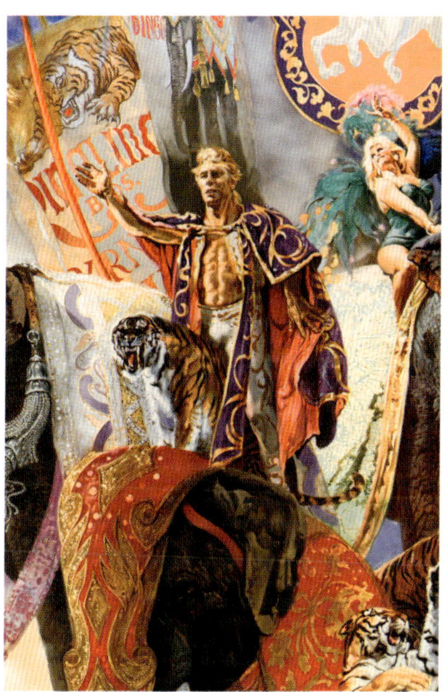

***The Greatest Show on Earth*, detail of Gunther Gebel-Williams**
Gunther Gebel-Williams was one of the most celebrated animal trainers in circus history.

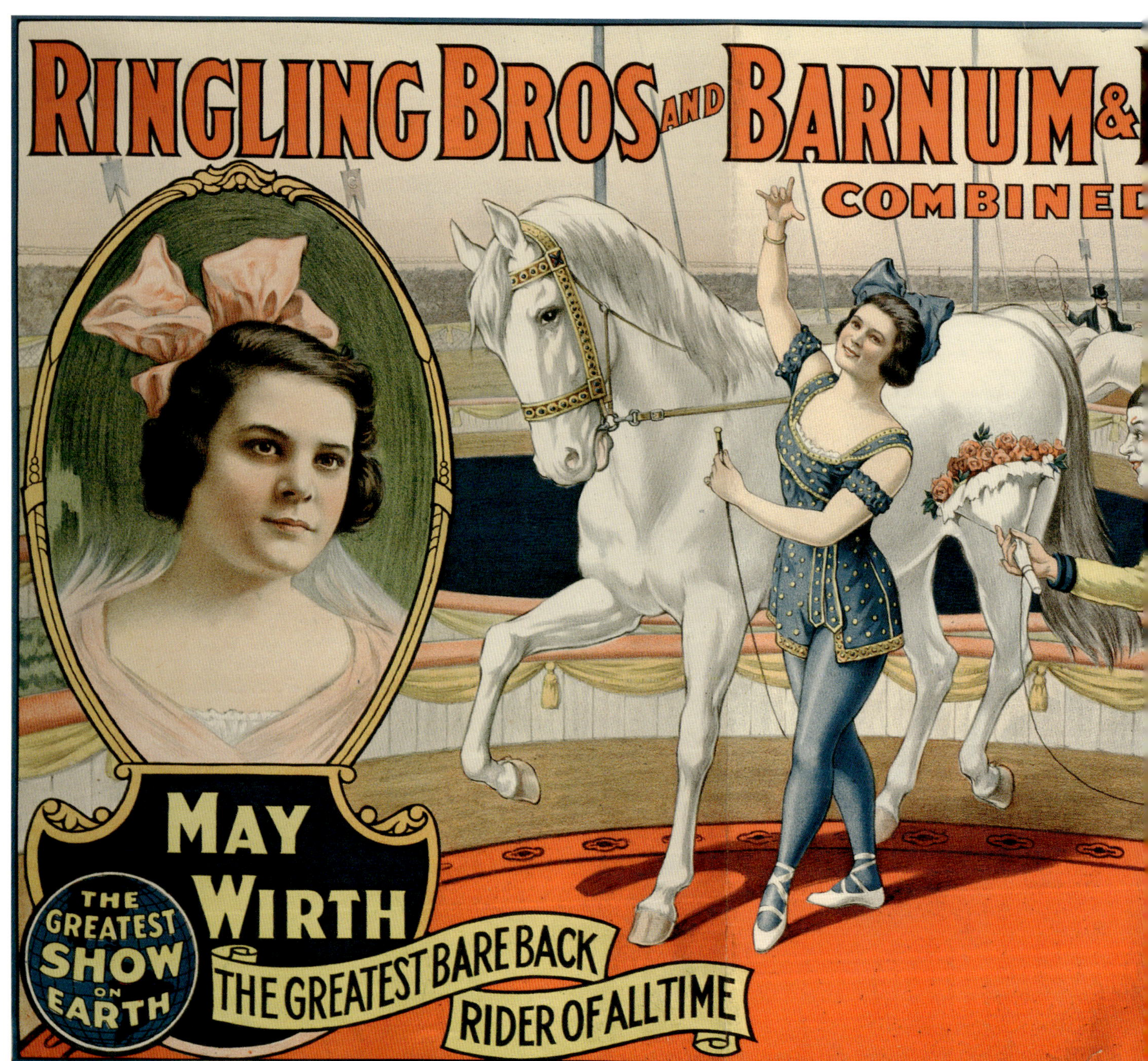
RINGLING BROS AND BARNUM &
COMBINED
MAY
WIRTH
THE GREATEST SHOW ON EARTH
THE GREATEST BARE BACK
RIDER OF ALL TIME

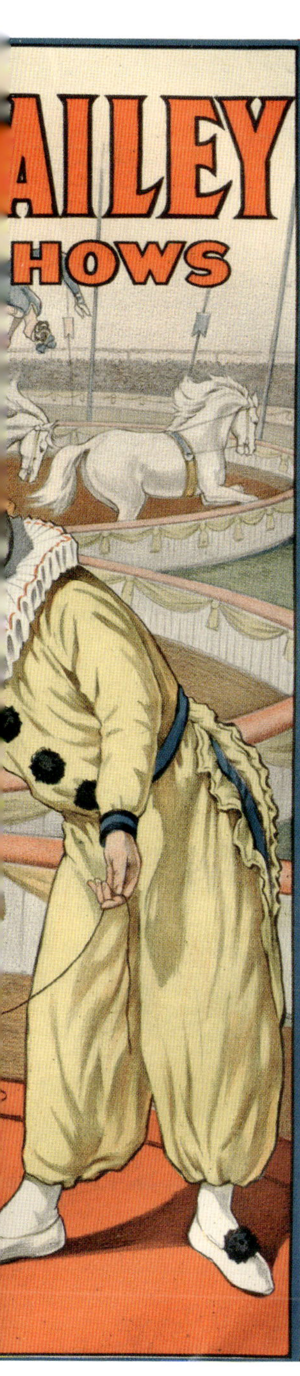

Strobridge Lithographing Company, Ringling Bros. and Barnum & Bailey Combined Shows poster, 1925
This poster features a portrait of legendary equestrienne May Wirth.

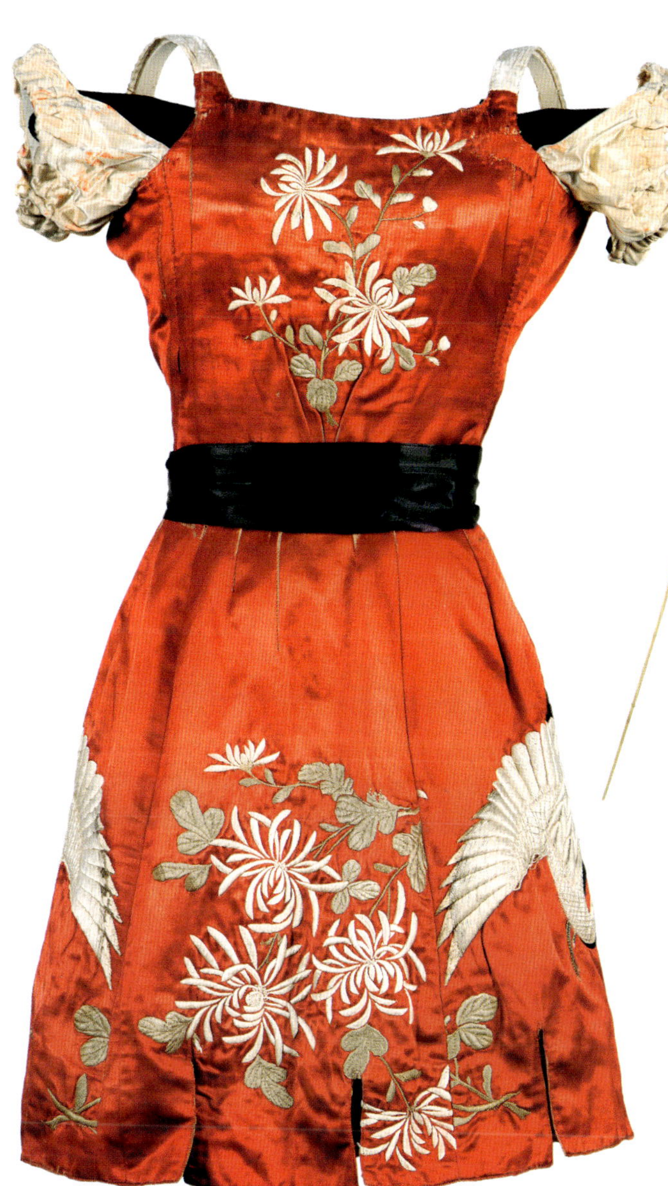

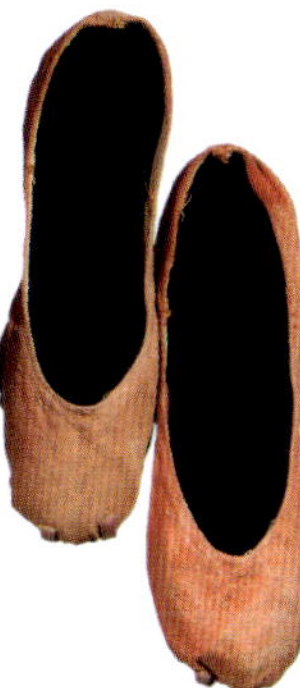

May Wirth's riding costume, early twentieth century

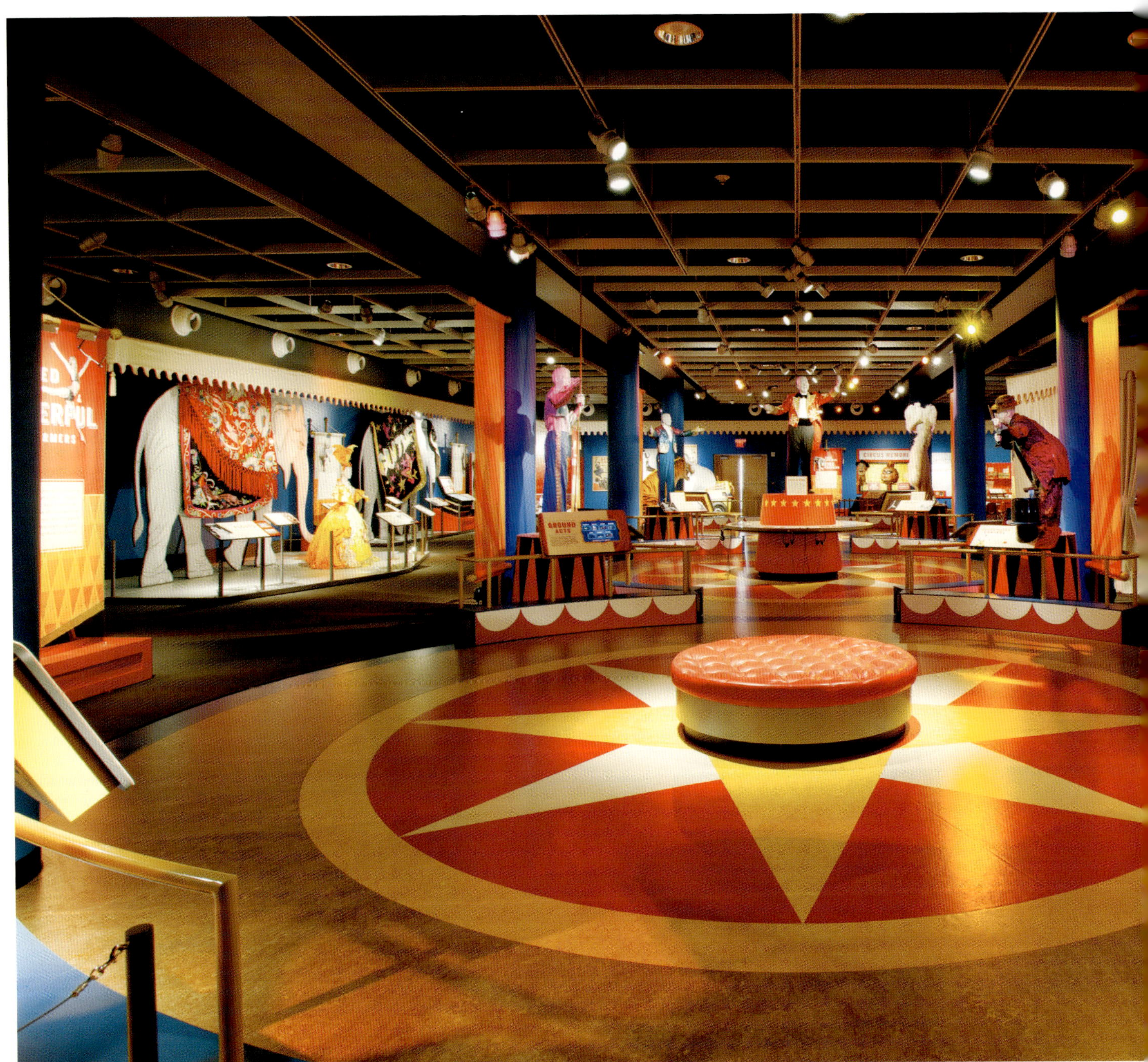
GROUND
ACTS

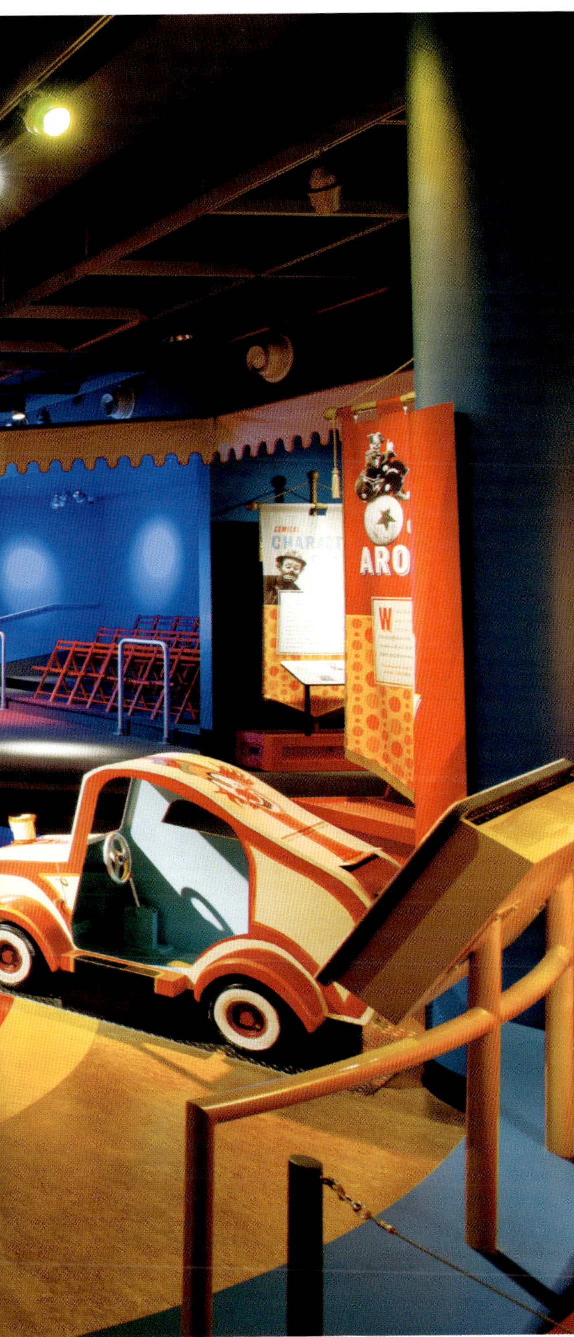

Interactive gallery in the Tibbals Learning Center

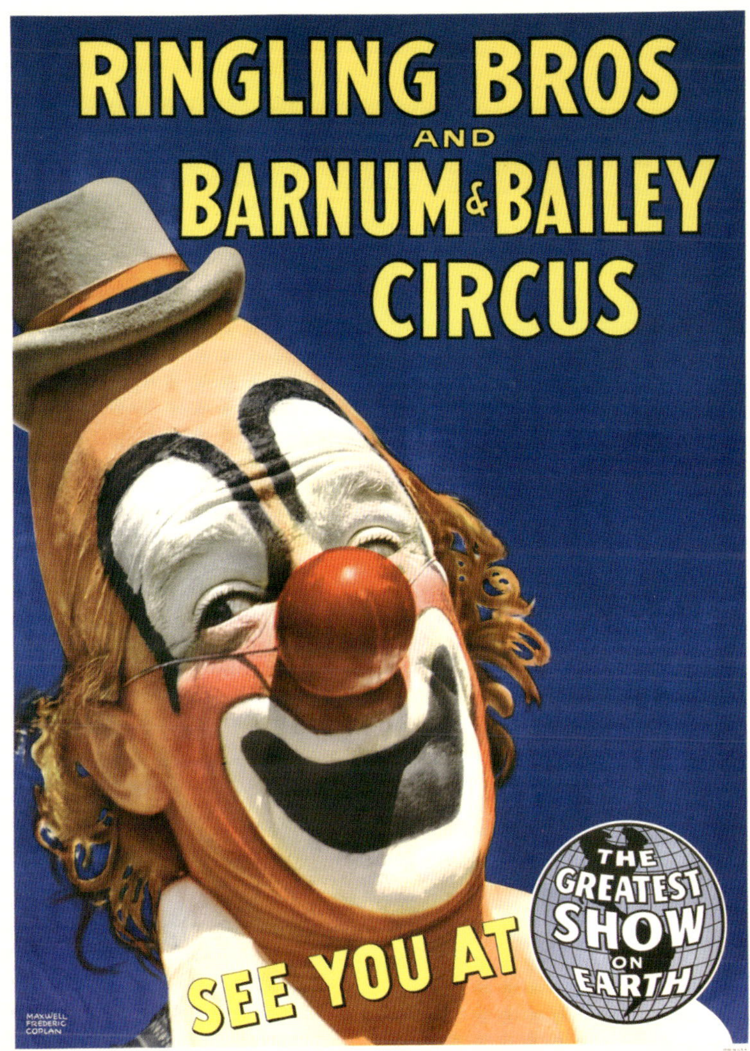

Maxwell Frederic Coplan, Ringling Bros. and Barnum & Bailey Circus poster, 1944
This poster features famous clown Lou Jacobs, whose miniature clown car is a highlight of the circus collection.

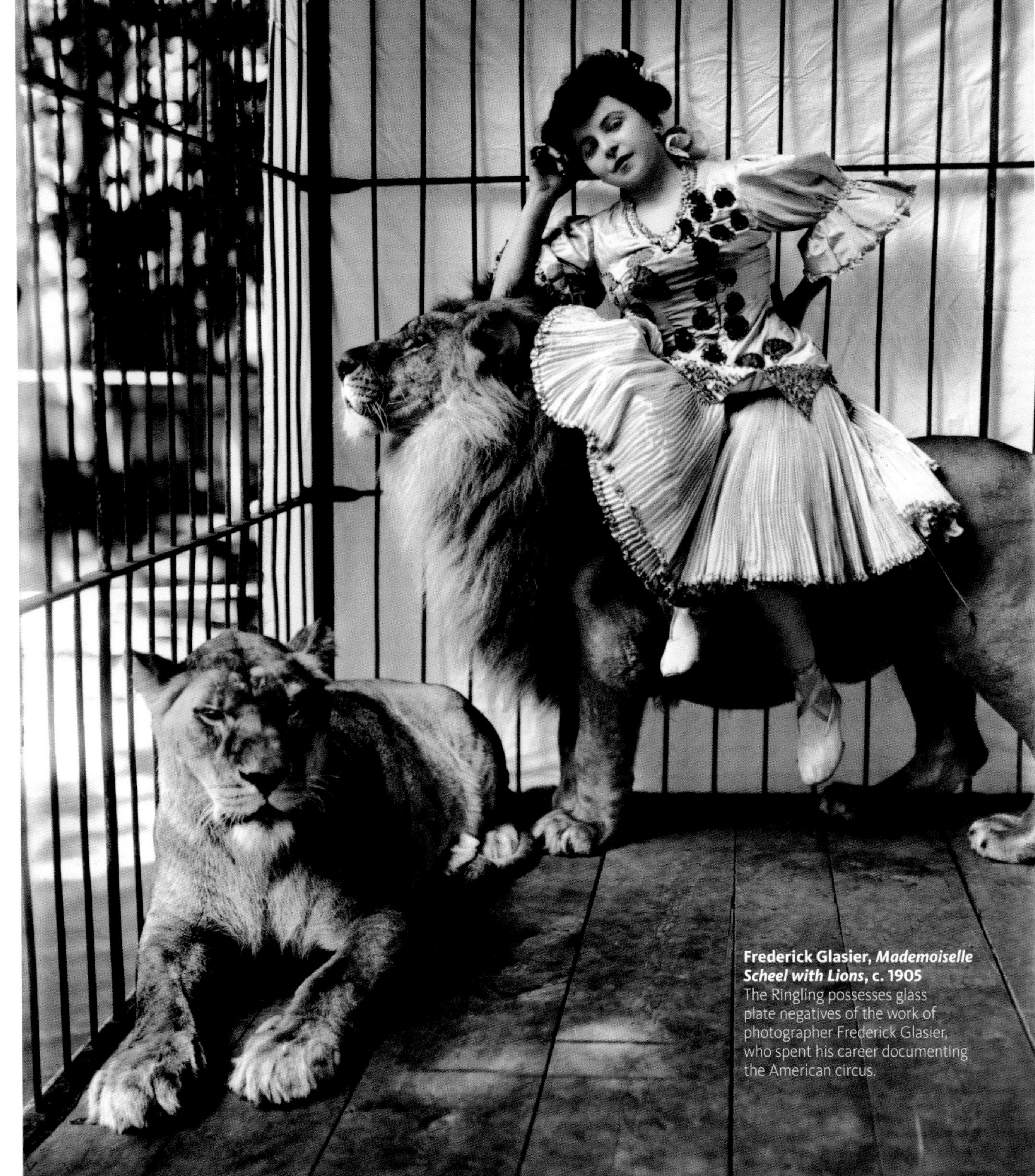

Frederick Glasier, *Mademoiselle Scheel with Lions*, c. 1905
The Ringling possesses glass plate negatives of the work of photographer Frederick Glasier, who spent his career documenting the American circus.

WINTER QUARTERS

John Ringling moved the winter quarters of the Ringling Bros. and Barnum & Bailey Circus to Sarasota in 1927. Winter quarters consisted of practice areas, workshops, and railroad yards occupying 200 acres of former fairgrounds. It became a major tourist attraction, drawing hundreds of thousands of visitors, who flocked to see performers rehearse and animals train in preparation for the season ahead.

While winter quarters relocated to Venice, Florida, in 1960, Sarasota remains the home of many circus families and retains the title of "Circus City, USA."

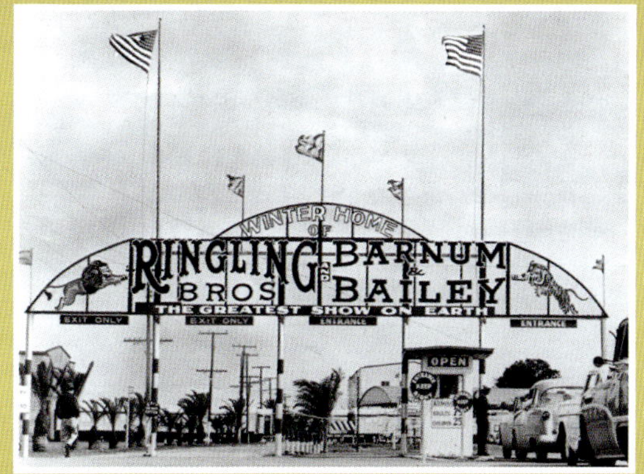

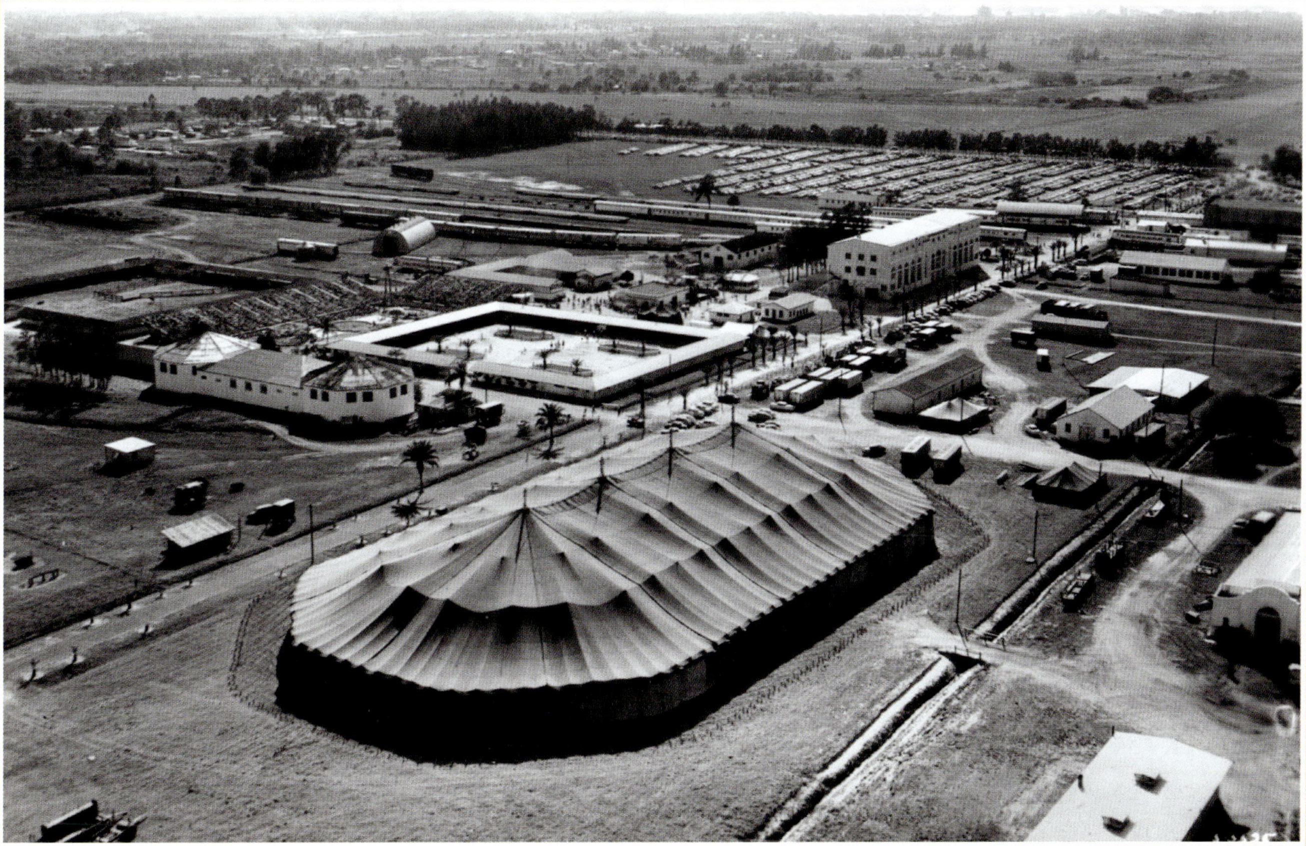

Winter quarters, c. 1950

Entrance to winter quarters, c. 1945

HISTORIC ASOLO THEATER

The Historic Asolo Theater was built in Asolo, Italy, in 1798. It was installed in the great hall of a palace built in the fifteenth century for Caterina Cornaro, the exiled queen of Cyprus.

The theater consisted of a U-shaped structure of three tiers, decorated with painted medallions and gilded ornaments. It was remodeled in 1857 and later dismantled in 1931. The space was converted into a cinema named in honor of acclaimed actress Eleonora Duse, who had performed at the theater in 1885.

Art dealer Adolph Loewi subsequently acquired the theater. Through the efforts of his friend, Chick Austin, The Ringling purchased it in 1949 for $8,000. It was

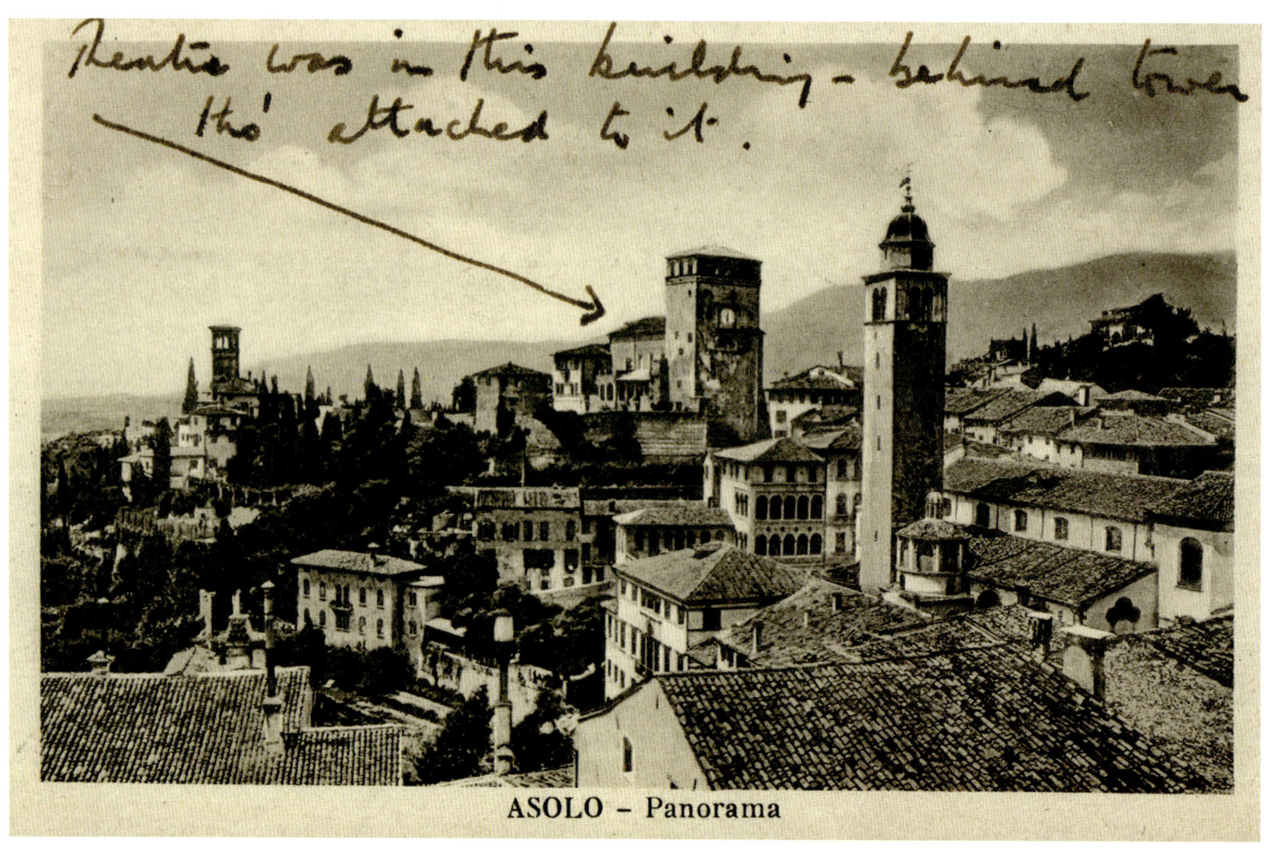

Postcard from Asolo, Italy, 1940s
The arrow drawn by the sender points to the original location of the theater.

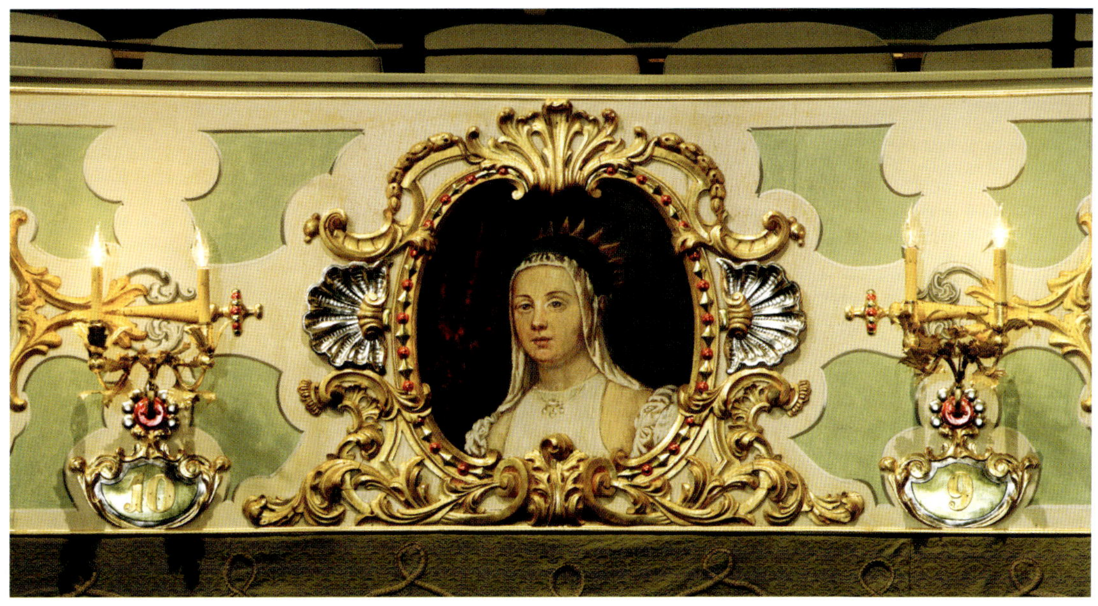

Caterina Cornaro, queen of Cyprus
Positioned above the "royal box," this portrait faces the stage of the Historic Asolo Theater.

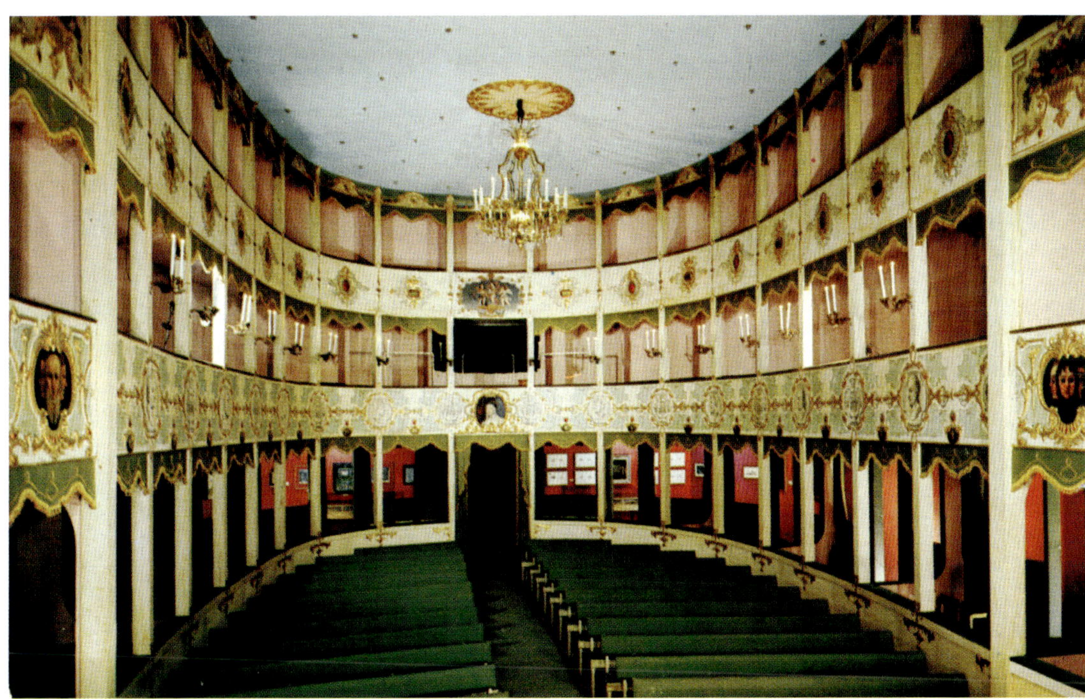

Postcard of the Historic Asolo Theater, 1952
The theater is shown here as it appeared in the Museum of Art.

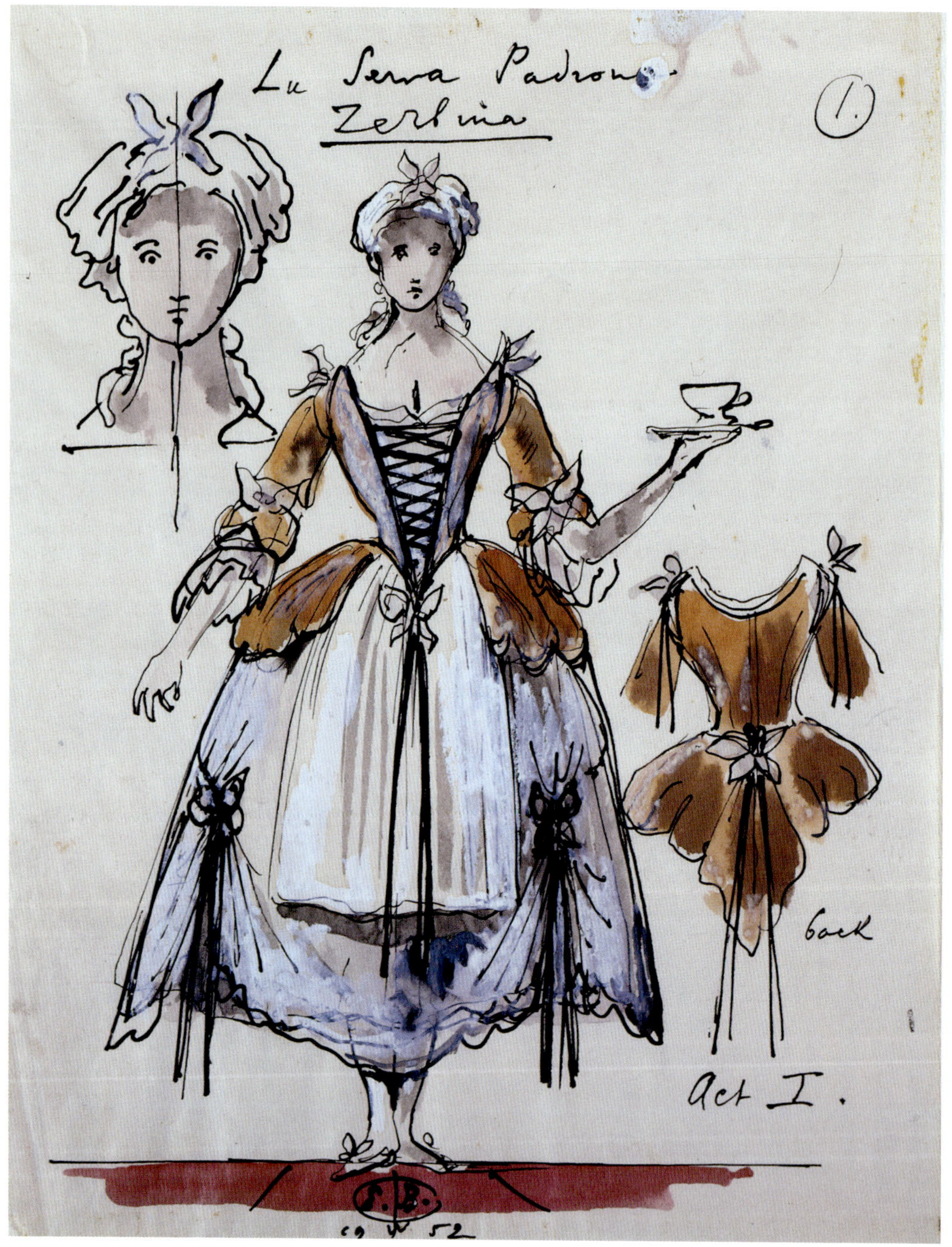

Eugene Berman, costume design for *La Serva Padrona*, 1952
The opera *La Serva Padrona* by composer Giovanni Battista Pergolesi was performed at the opening of the Historic Asolo Theater in 1952.

Eugene Berman, set design for *La Serva Padrona*, 1952
Eugene Berman was a famous designer for ballets and operas.

installed in a gallery of the Museum of Art, where it opened in 1952.

Architect Marion Manley designed a new building to house the theater in 1954. The opening night performance in 1958 was followed by a celebration at Ca' d'Zan, which was featured in *LIFE* magazine. Guests wore costumes lent for the occasion by the Ringling Bros. and Barnum & Bailey Circus.

In time, the theater became the birthplace of local performing arts institutions, including the Sarasota Opera and Asolo Repertory Theatre. It fell into disrepair after the departure of its resident companies in the 1980s. Following an extensive restoration, it opened in its current location in the Visitor Pavilion in 2006.

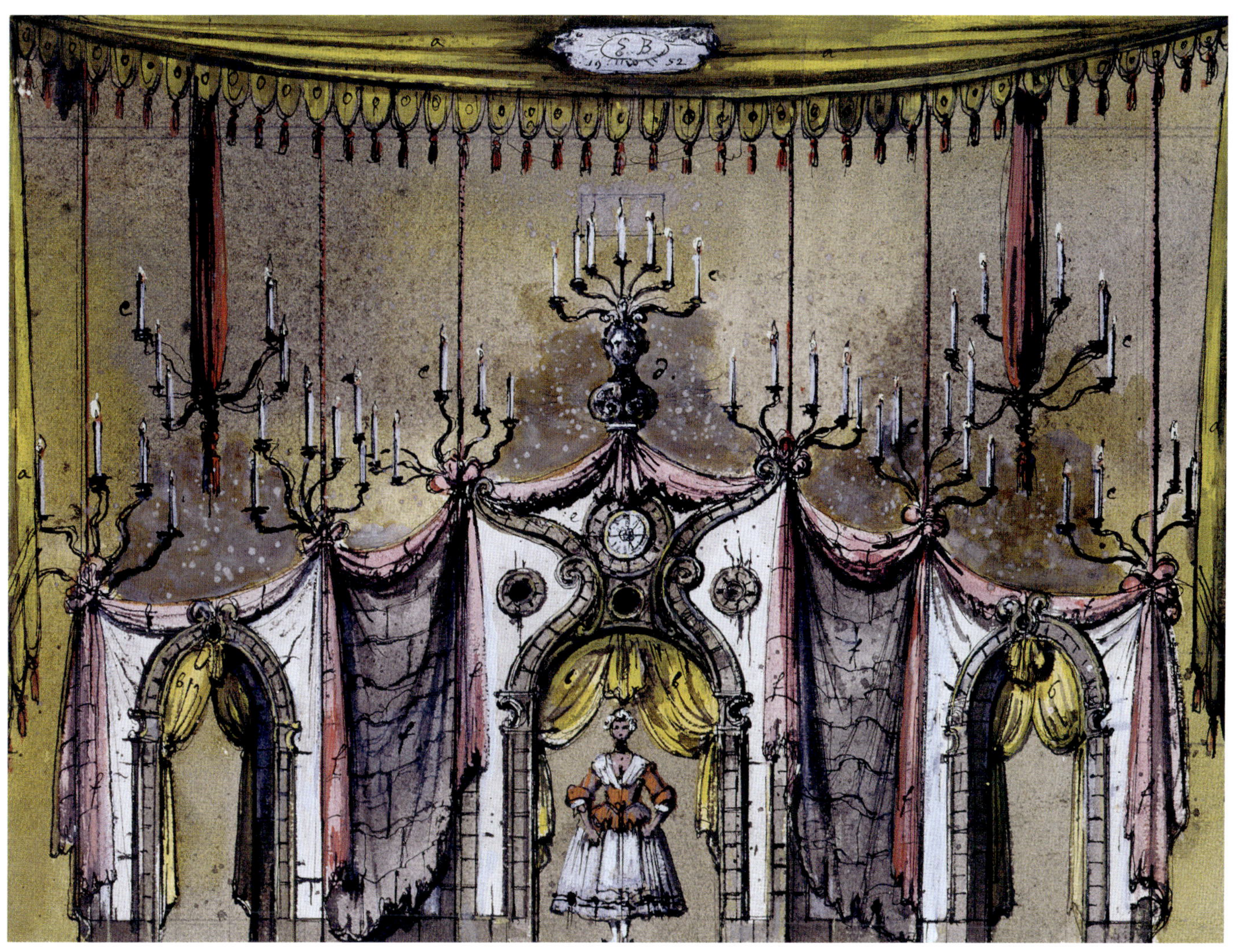

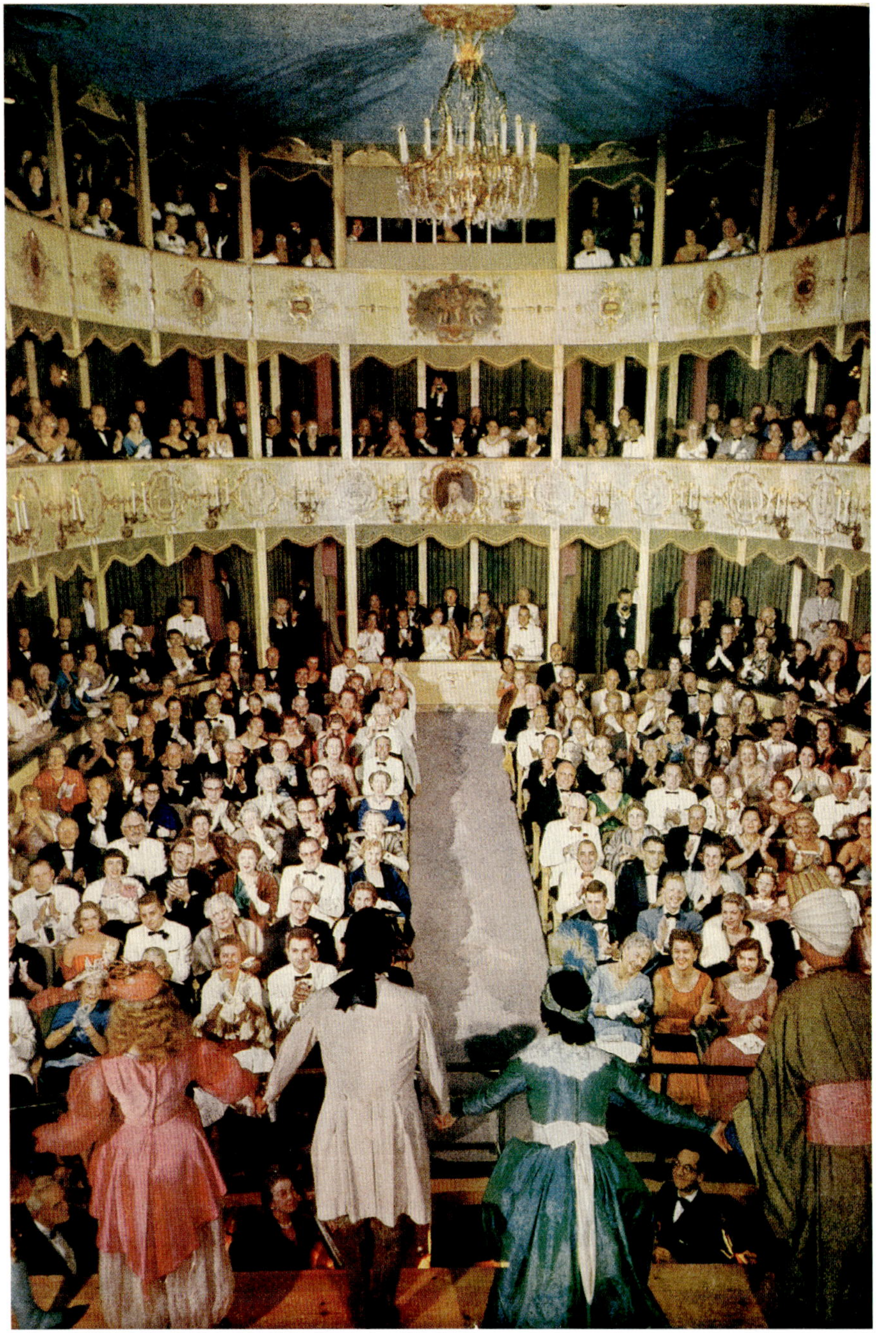

Opening night of the Historic Asolo Theater, 1958
This photograph was featured in *LIFE* magazine.

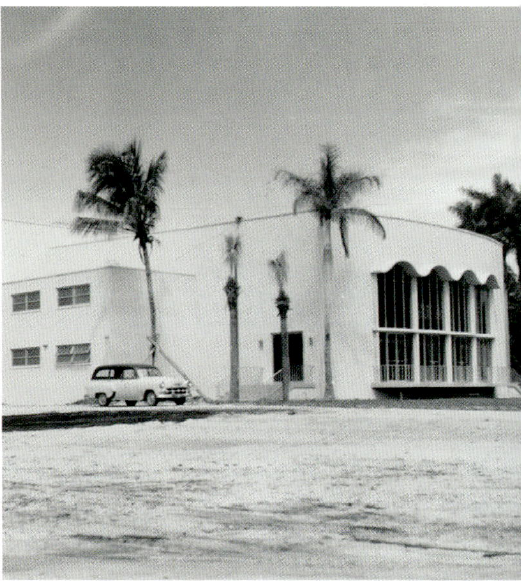

Historic Asolo Theater, 1957
This photograph was sent to Chick Austin while construction on the theater was nearing completion.

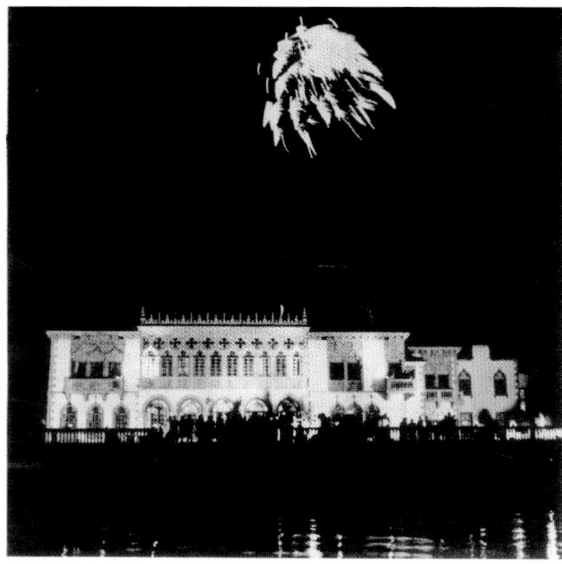

FIREWORKS BURST ABOVE RINGLING MANSION IN SARASOTA AS GUESTS WATCH FROM BAYSIDE TERRACE

SARASOTA SPECTACLE

Theater brought from Venice opens with opera

In Sarasota, Fla., home of circuses, the Ringling Museum of Art recently put on a party that sparkled with the pageantry of the great showmen. The affair began with an opera, *The Abduction from the Seraglio*, performed to celebrate the formal opening of the Asolo Theater (*opposite page*). The theater was built near Venice in the 18th Century but dismantled in 1930. Florida bought it several years ago for use on the Venetian-styled John Ringling estate which the circus magnate gave the state.

After the opera, guests drove to the Ringling mansion where they spent the rest of the evening dancing in tapestried splendor and being entertained by fireworks, jugglers and acrobats. Couples swept around a ballroom which was strung with gaudy streamers and brightened by borrowed circus decorations. During the last dance a guest, admiring the spectacle, said, "John Ringling would have loved this."

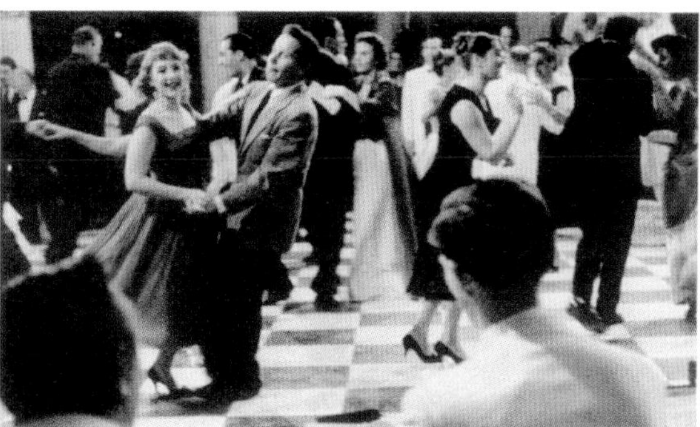

POLKA DANCING in great hall finds New York City Opera soprano Jacquelynne Moody and tenor Robert Rounseville (*left center*) taking lively part.

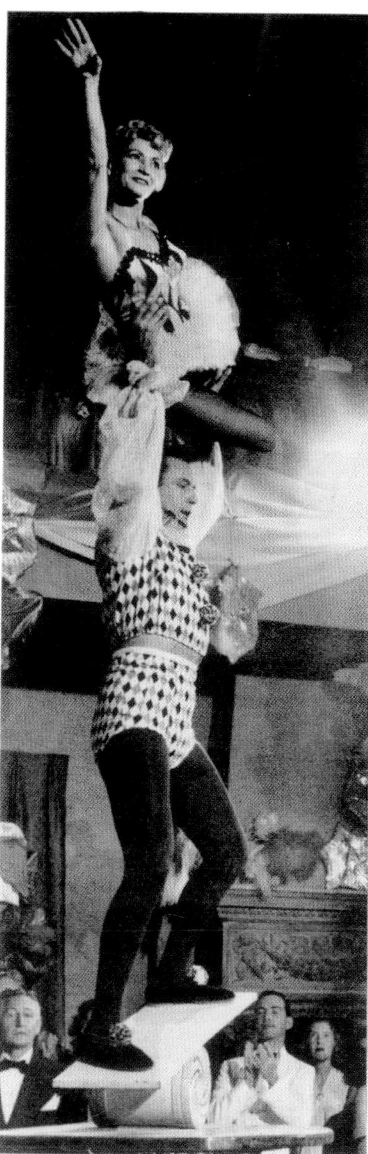

ACROBATIC ENTERTAINMENT carrying out Venetian theme is provided by members of Christiani Brothers Circus who do hazardous balancing act.

Article from *LIFE* magazine, 1958

Historic Asolo Theater today

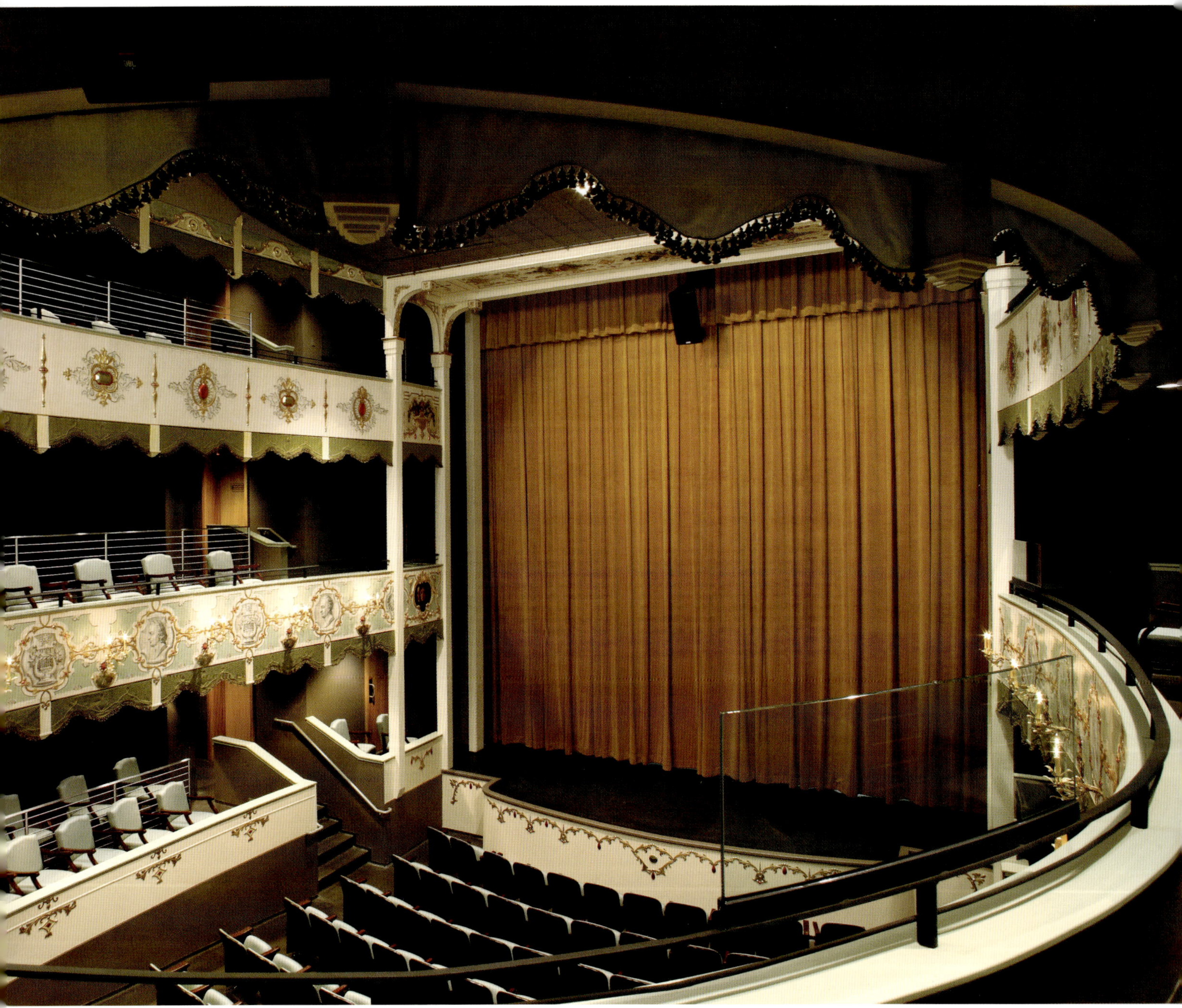

ASOLO REPERTORY THEATRE

Theater faculty from Florida State University started a summer acting festival in 1960 held in the Historic Asolo Theater. The festival became a professional theater company six years later. The company eventually outgrew its original venue and moved across the street in 1989 to new premises, known as the Asolo (now FSU) Center for the Performing Arts. The company is joined there by the FSU/Asolo Conservatory for Actor Training, one of the top programs of its type in the nation. Students perform as part of the company in their third and final year, gaining professional experience along with a Master of Fine Arts degree.

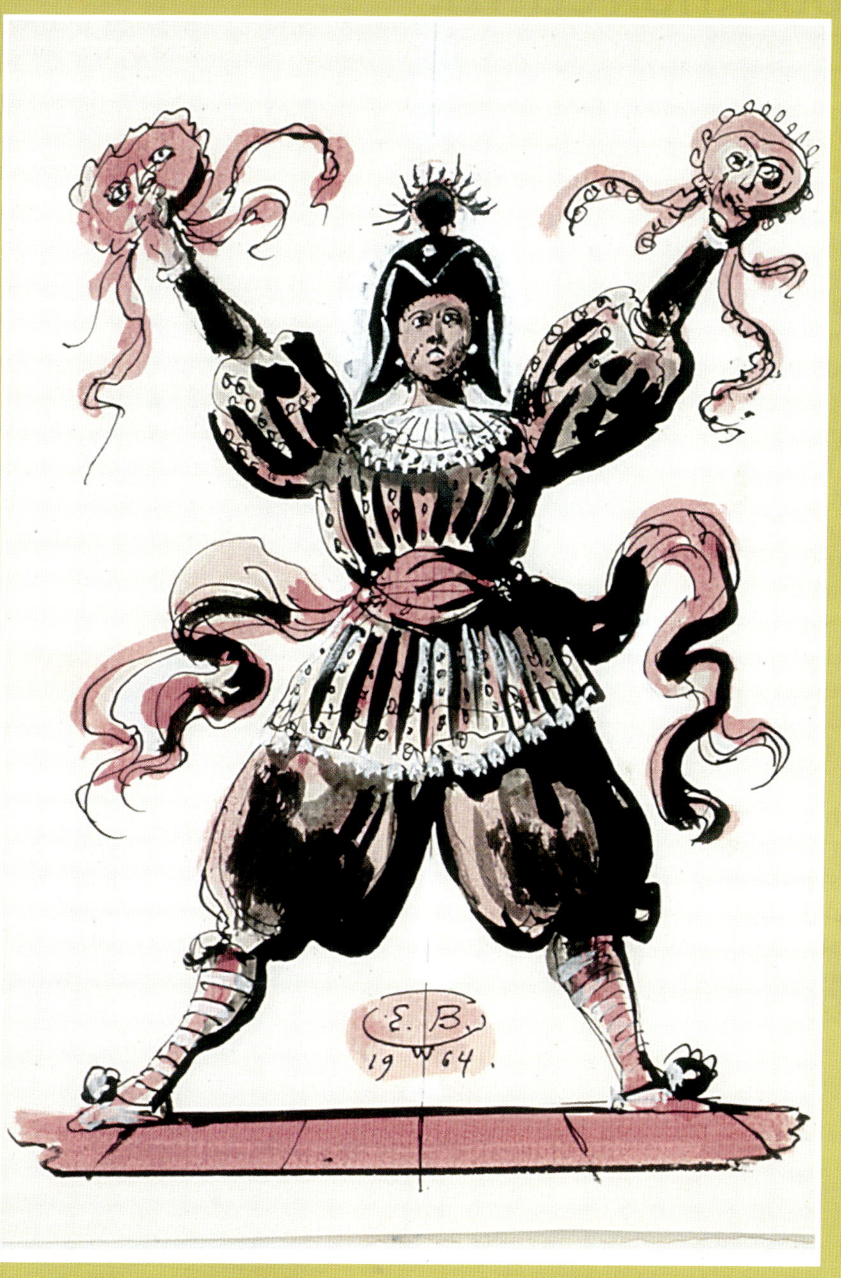

Eugene Berman, *Asolo Theater Insignia: Costumed Male Figure*, 1964
This insignia was associated with both the theater and company that performed there.

EDUCATION CENTER

The Education Center, opened in 2006, houses staff offices, a classroom, and conservation laboratory where works from the collections are carefully preserved for the benefit of future generations. Research in the laboratory helps to determine how works are made, why they deteriorate, and what the best methods are to repair and maintain them.

The center also accommodates The Ringling Art Library, one of the largest resources of its type in the southeastern United States. The library contains approximately 60,000 volumes from the sixteenth to twenty-first centuries, on subjects such as art, art history, architecture, fashion, and theater. It features a number of special collections, including some 800 books that belonged to John Ringling.

John's books reflect his various interests. Some relate to the places he traveled, while others were used to expand his knowledge of art history, which, in turn, helped to inform his activities as a collector. Many have fine bindings, which are the subject of an ongoing restoration project. All are stored in a special room of the library, where they are accessible by appointment.

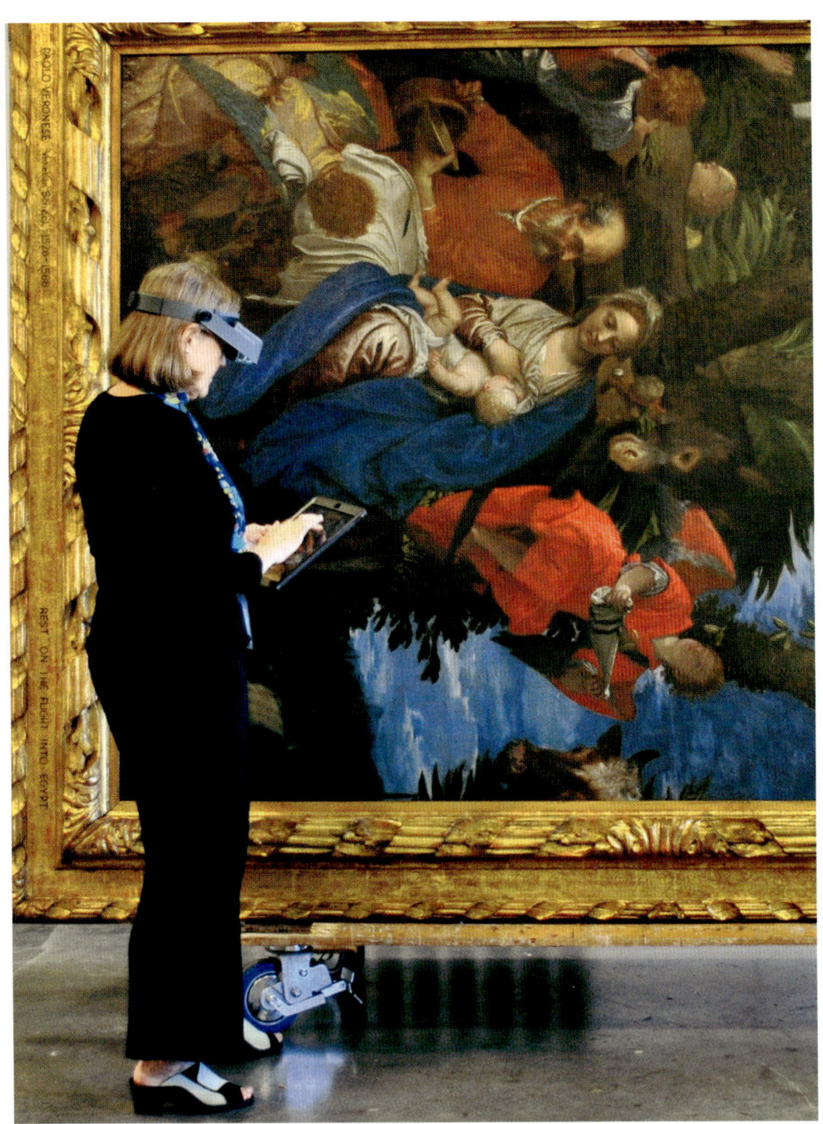

Conservator at work

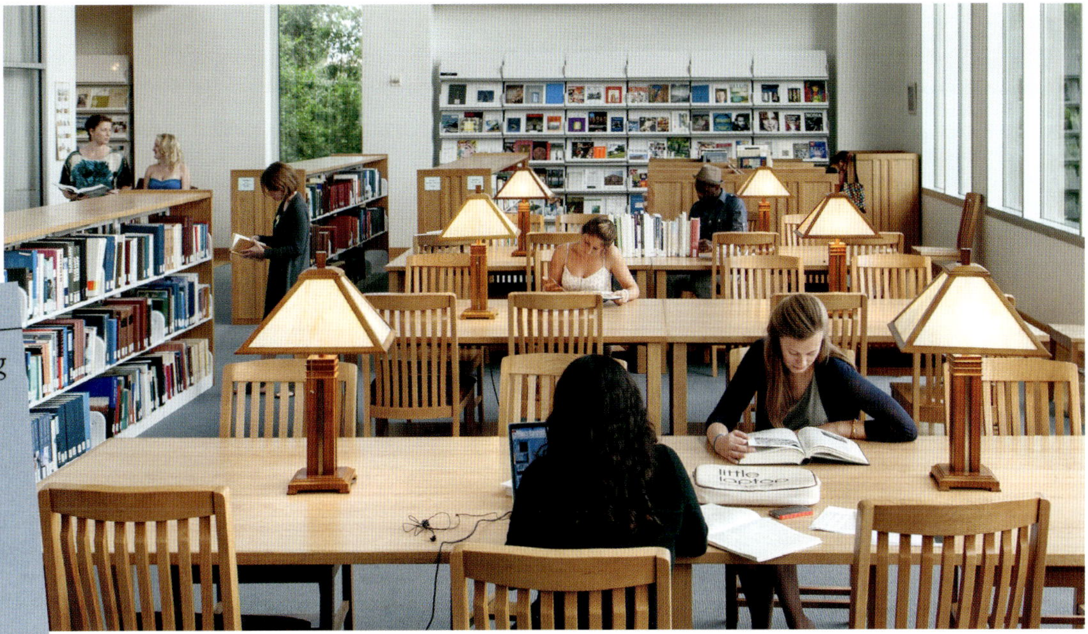

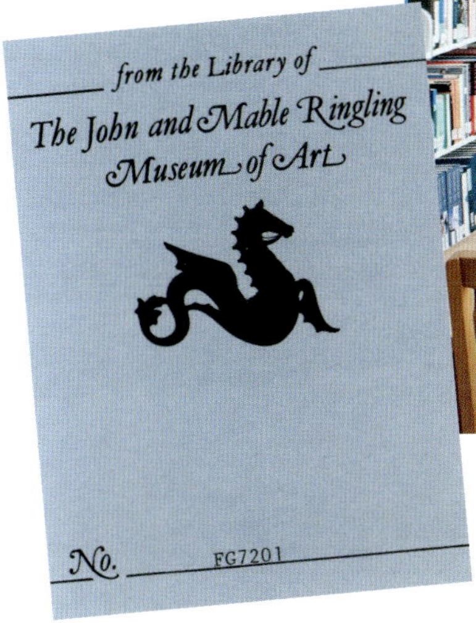

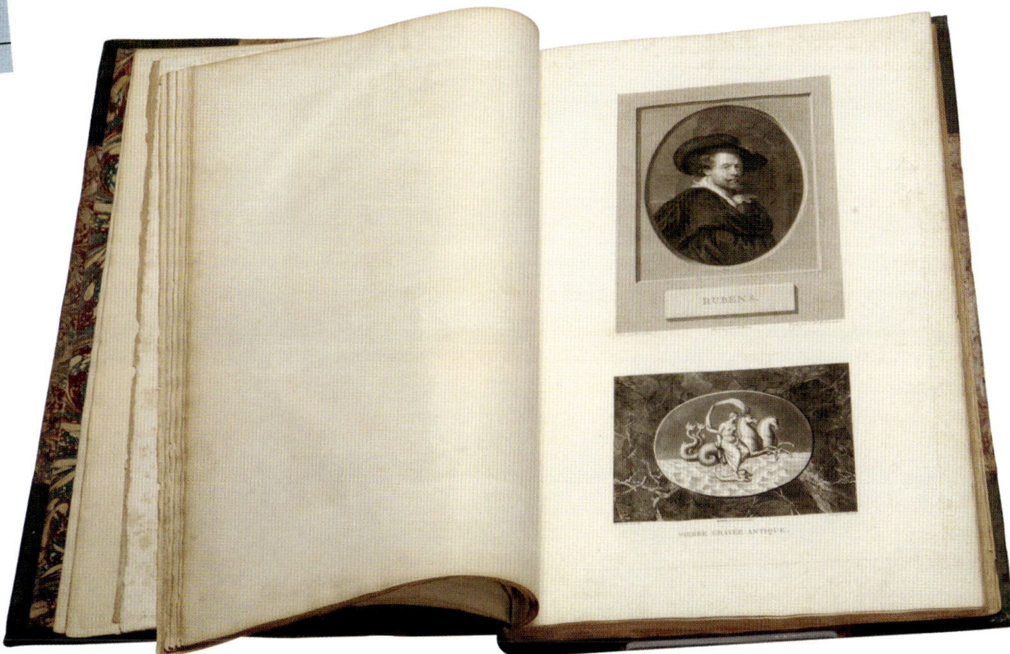

The Ringling Art Library
The library is open to students, scholars, and the public.

Bookplate from The Ringling Art Library
The hippocampus, or mythical seahorse, on this bookplate is based on an ornament from a gondola owned by Mable Ringling.

Rare book belonging to John Ringling, 1807
This book is open to a page with a portrait of artist Peter Paul Rubens, whose work is a highlight of John Ringling's collection of paintings.

BAYFRONT GARDENS

The Ringling occupies sixty-six acres of grounds on the shores of Sarasota Bay. The grounds include gardens and other natural elements, some of which date from the Ringlings' day.

To the east of Ca' d'Zan is Mable Ringling's Rose Garden, founded in 1913. Covering 27,000 square feet, the garden is laid out in a formal design that Mable had likely seen on trips to Italy.

To the north of Ca' d'Zan is the Secret Garden where Mable grew "onesies and twosies" given to her as gifts by family and friends. Beyond the garden is a private enclosure where the Ringlings are buried together with John's sister, Ida.

Mable Ringling with roses, c. 1905
Mable Ringling was an avid gardener. She was elected the first president of the Founders Circle of the Sarasota Garden Club in 1927.

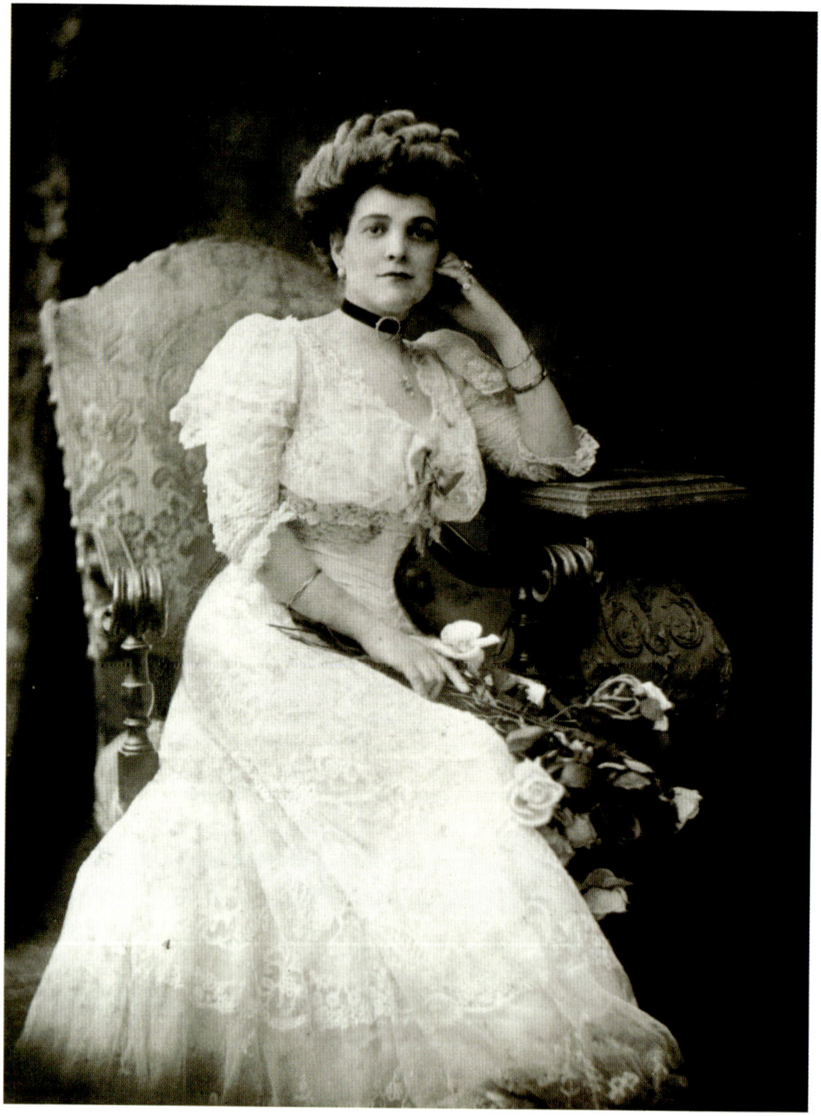

Statue in the rose garden

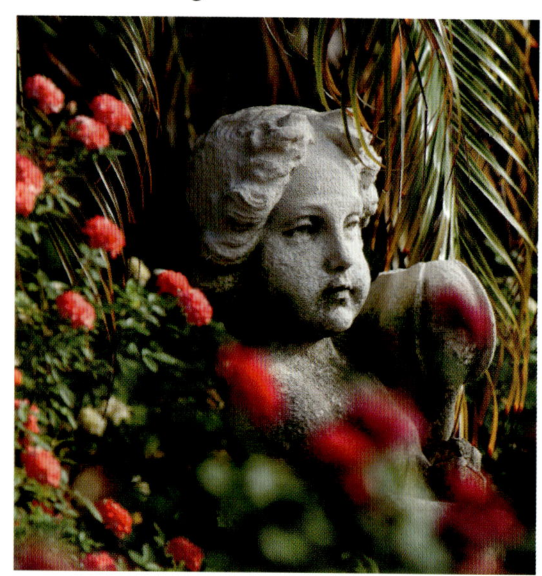

Mable Ringling's Rose Garden
Though none of Mable Ringling's original rosebushes survive, many of the 1,200 roses currently growing in the garden are of the same varieties as those she planted.

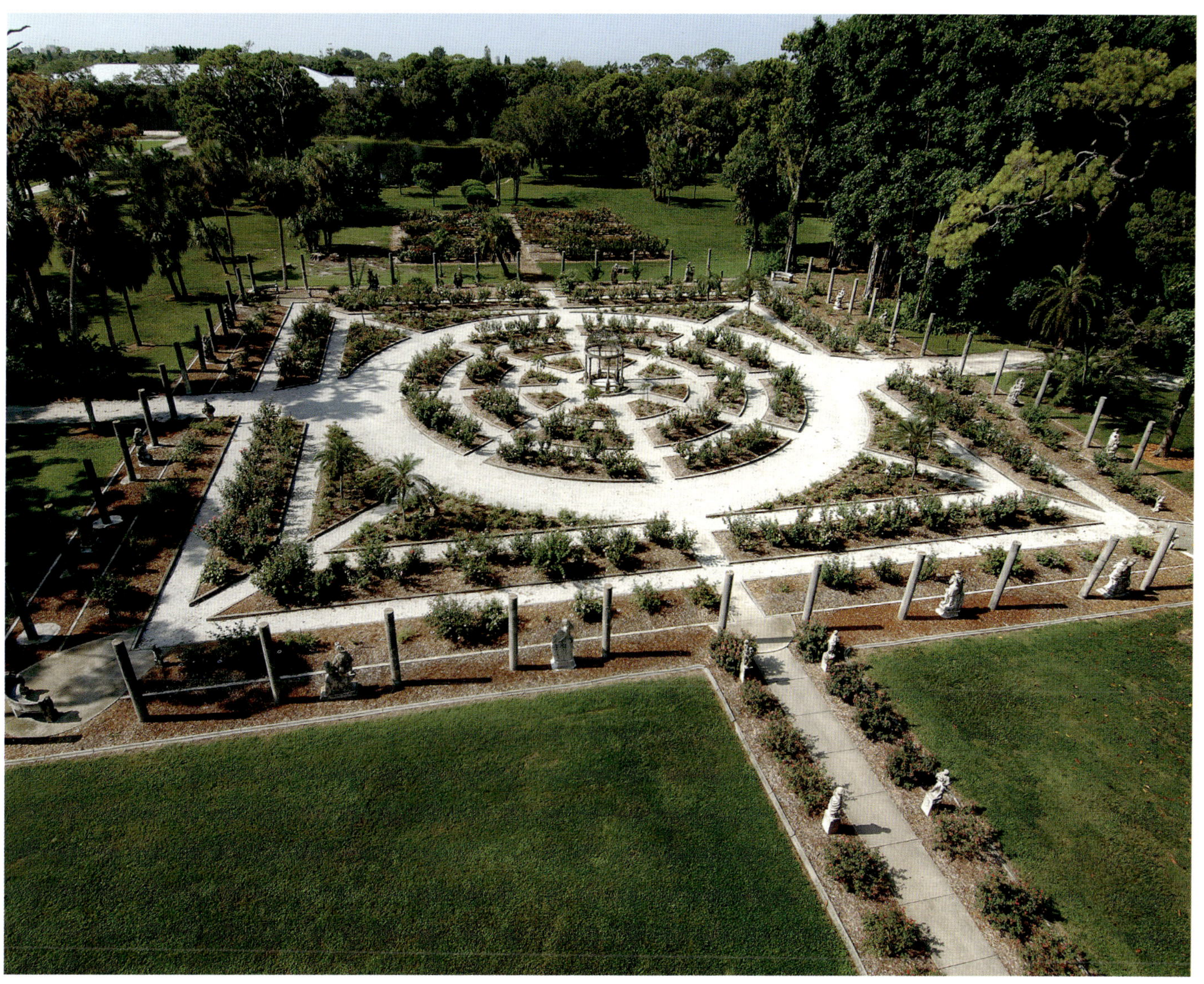

Secret Garden, 1920s
Mable Ringling relaxed in this peaceful spot between her many social and civic engagements.

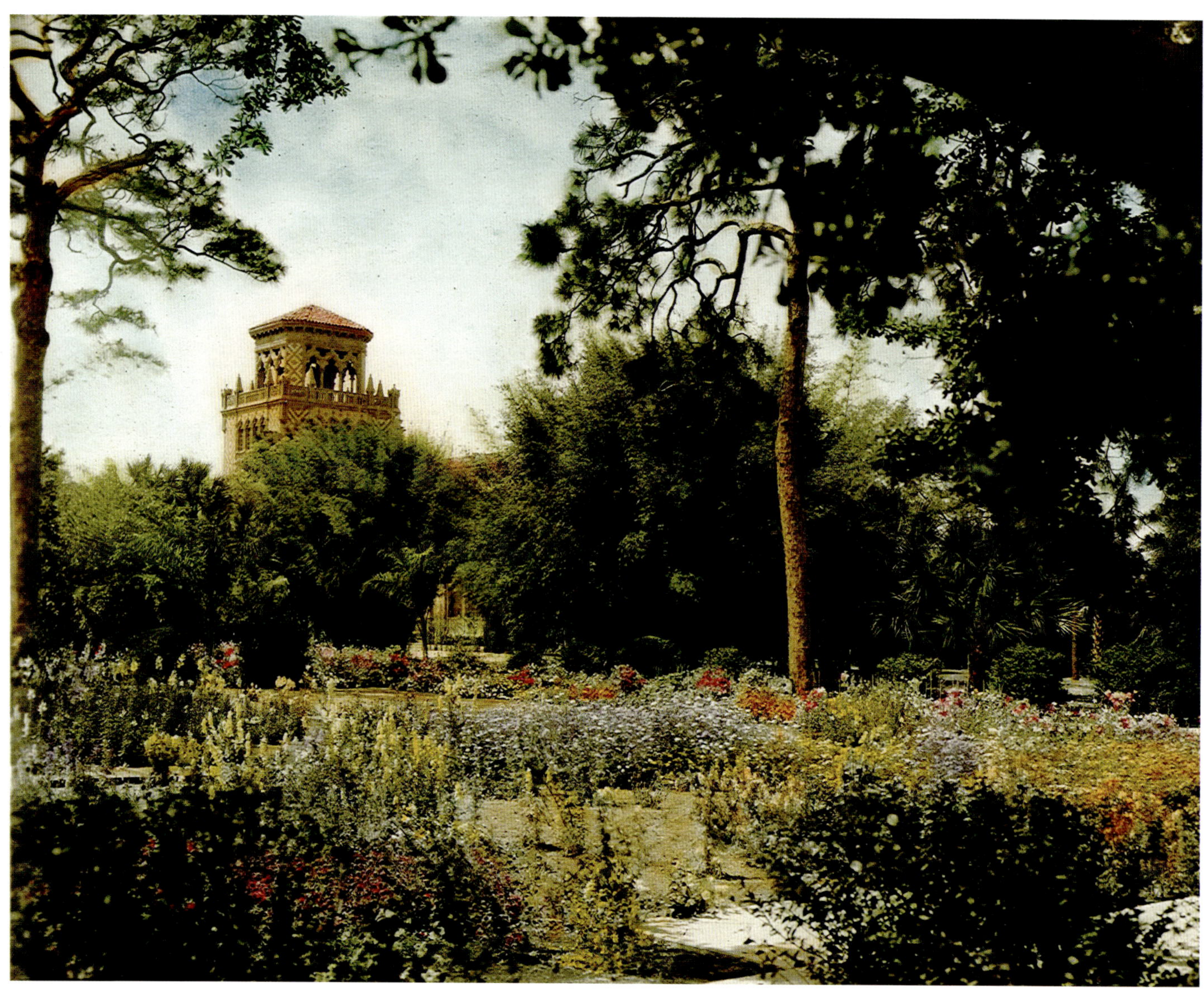

Postcard of the Dwarf Garden, c. 1958
The garden is shown here between the Museum of Art and the building then housing the Historic Asolo Theater.

Dwarf Garden today
The garden moved to its current location in 2006.

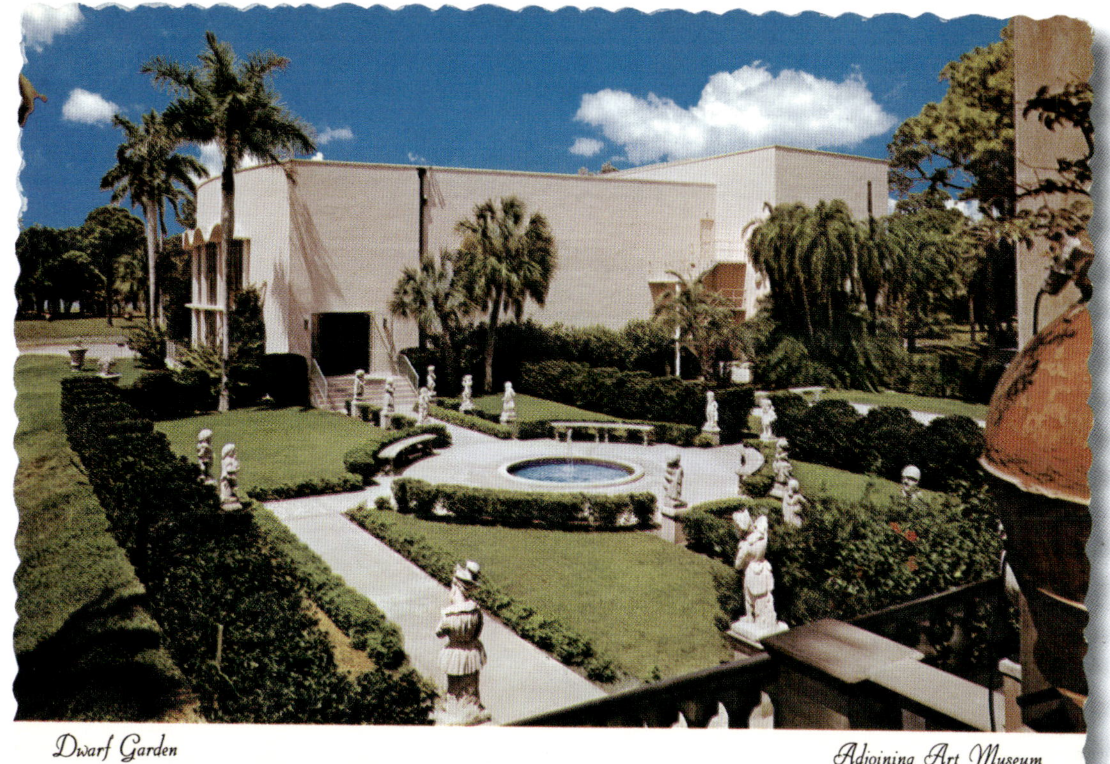

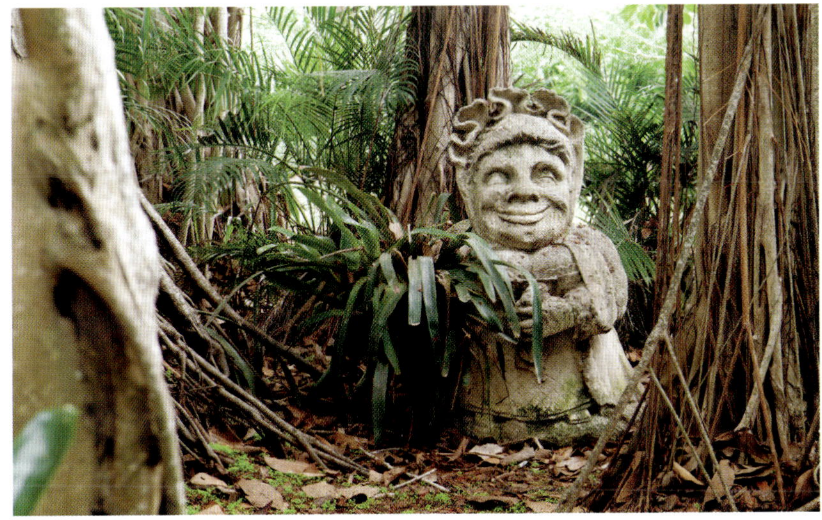

To the south of the Visitor Pavilion is the Dwarf Garden, named after a series of stone statues of comical characters found there. Acquired by John in Italy in 1925, the statues continue to delight visitors young and old.

Throughout the grounds are thousands of trees, including exotic species with unusual names such as dinner plate, monkey puzzle, and shaving brush. The most impressive of these are the banyans, which legend has it were given to John by his friend, Thomas Edison.

A selection of local and regional types line the Millennium Tree Trail on the southern edge of the property, established to mark the year 2000. The trees are planted in native habitats ranging from swampy to coastal.

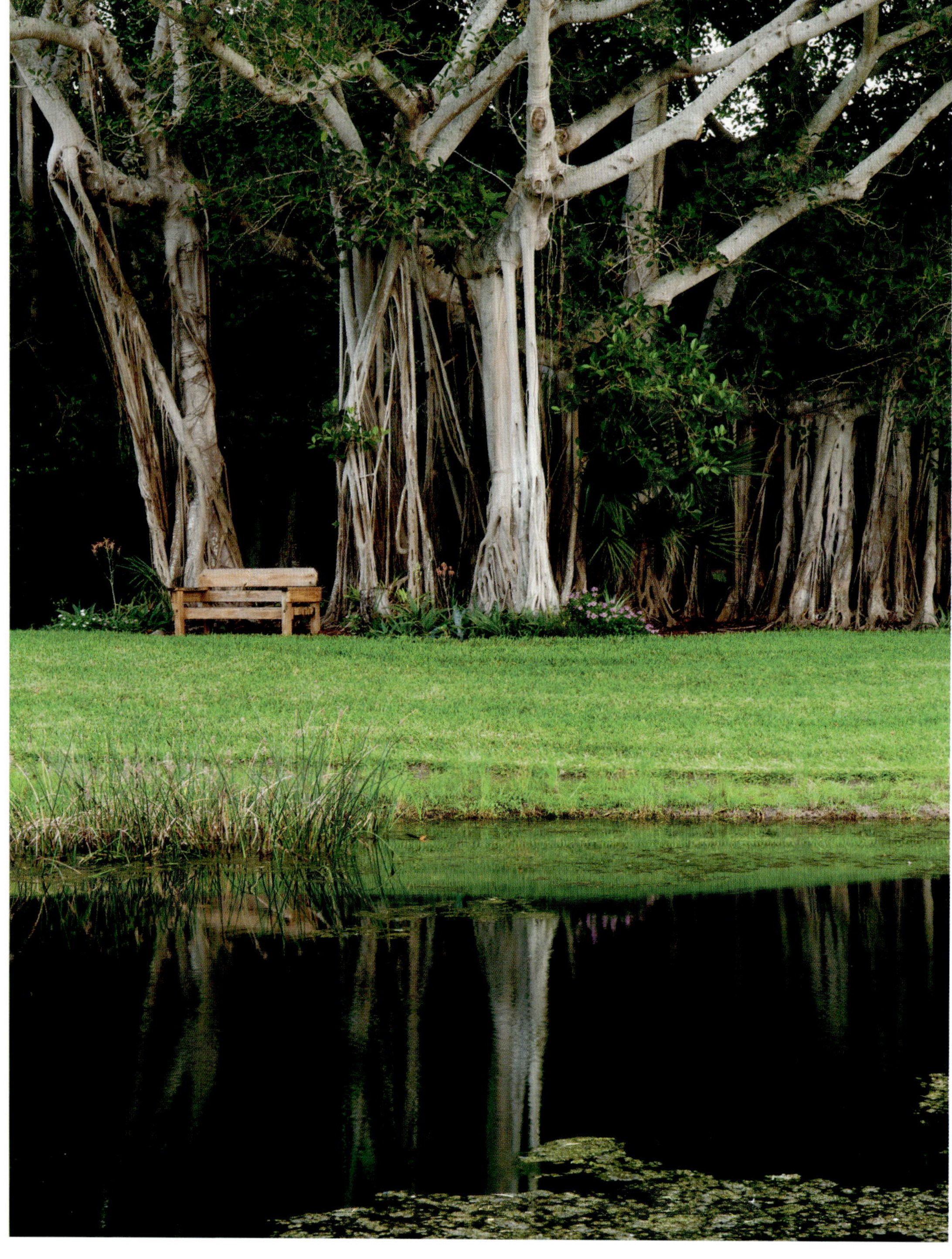

Banyan tree
Native to India and Pakistan, banyan trees are notable for their massive size.

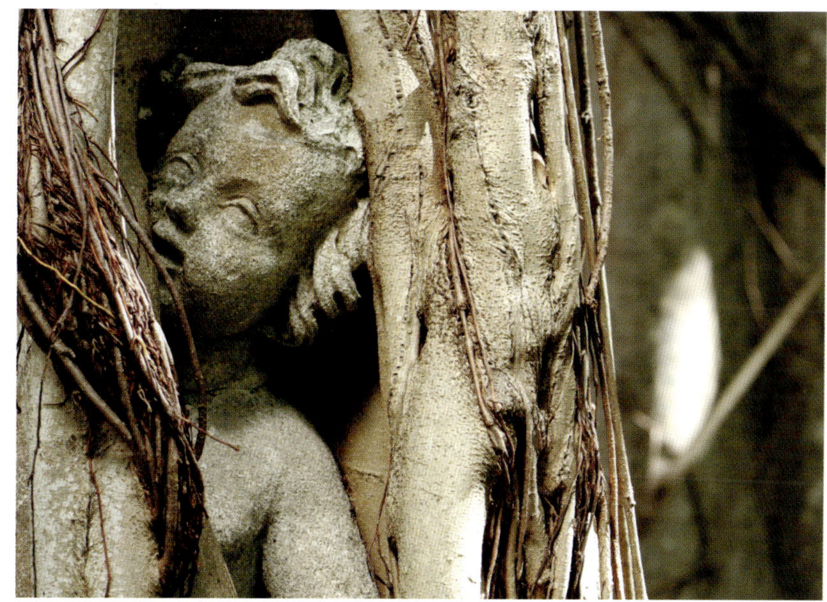

Four large ponds keep the grounds properly drained, particularly in the rainy summer months. The ponds are home to an abundance of wildlife, including fish, turtles, and birds.

The grounds have been enhanced in recent years by the Bolger Promenade and Campiello, used for public and private events. The newest addition to the grounds is the Bolger Playspace, opened in 2014, where children learn through play on equipment designed to engage the mind, enliven the body, and enrich the spirit.

Statue in a banyan tree
Visitors enjoy discovering this statue hidden among the roots of a banyan tree.

Anhinga on a statue
Anhinga can be seen drying their feathers in the sun, occasionally perched on the heads of statues.

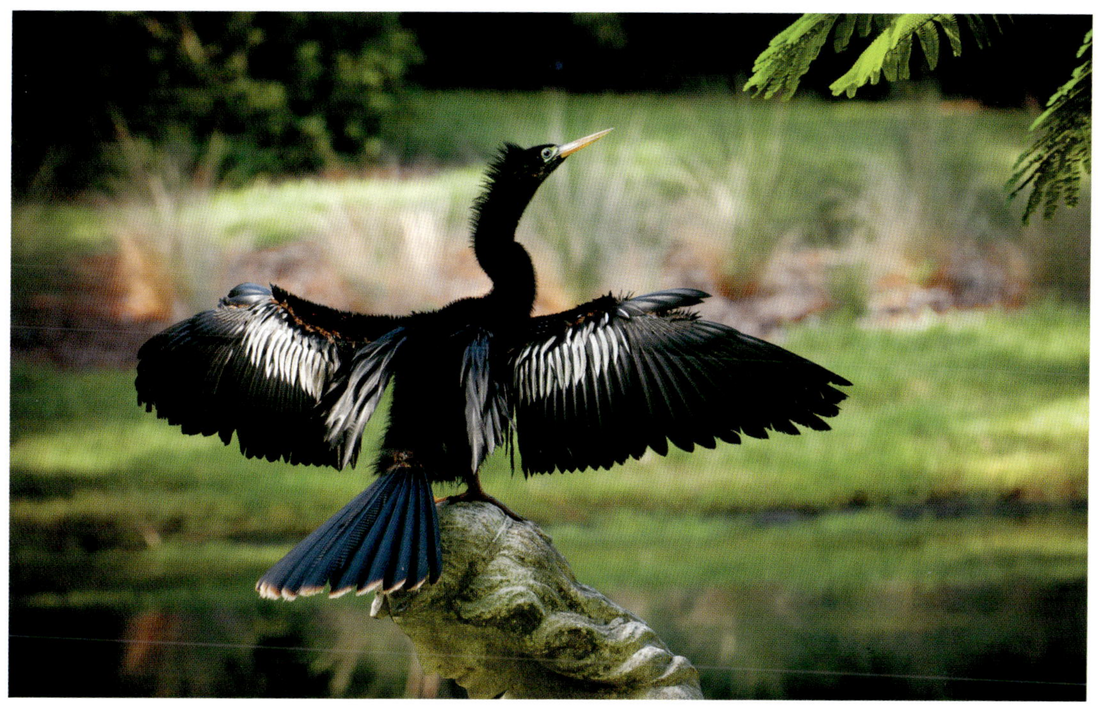

First published in 2014 by Scala Arts & Heritage Publishers Ltd
10 Lion Yard, Tremadoc Road
London SW4 7NQ, UK
Tel: +44 (0)207 808 1550
www.scalapublishers.com

In association with The John and Mable Ringling Museum of Art

ISBN: 978-1-85759-913-8

Edited by Stephanie Emerson
Designed by Nigel Soper
Printed in China

10 9 8 7 6 5 4 3 2 1

Page 2: John Ringling at Ca' d'Zan, 1927 © Bettmann/CORBIS
Page 2: Students painting in the Museum of Art, 1947 © State Archives of Florida, *Florida Memory*
Page 8: Opening day of Ca' d'Zan, 1946 © State Archives of Florida, *Florida Memory*
Page 13: Ca' d'Zan, 1927 © Bettmann/CORBIS
Page 31: James Turrell, *Joseph's Coat*, 2011 © James Turrell, photo by Giovanni Lunardi
Page 32: R. Luke DuBois, *Circus Sarasota: Dolly Jacobs*, 2014 © R. Luke DuBois

Front Cover: Monkey decoration from Ca' d'Zan; Statue from the Museum of Art;
Wagon from the circus collection
Inside Front Cover: Ca' d'Zan
Back Cover: Hippocampus ornaments from Mable Ringling's gondola
Inside Back Cover: Museum of Art
Page 1: Wagon display in the Tibbals Learning Center